# 100 Secret Social Media Marketing Tricks for 2019

The Best Strategies & Tips for Digital Marketing, YouTube and Instagram Used by the Top Influencers and Personal Brands (Beginners Guide)

*Written by Leslie Spanier*

purposes only. All effort has been executed to present accurate, up to date, and reliable, complete information. No warranties of any kind are declared or implied. Readers acknowledge that the author is not engaging in the rendering of legal, financial, medical or professional advice. The content within this book has been derived from various sources. Please consult a licensed professional before attempting any techniques outlined in this book.

By reading this document, the reader agrees that under no circumstances is the author responsible for any losses, direct or indirect, which are incurred as a result of the use of information contained within this document, including, but not limited to, — errors, omissions, or inaccuracies.

# Table of Contents

# Introduction

Welcome to 2019, the fourth industrial age; an era where the rules are on a whole different level. Disruptive technologies such as the internet, robotics, and artificial intelligence have infiltrated every core of our operation from commerce to banking to health, and even to the economic sector and believe me, they are evolving every day. No thanks to continuous innovation, the world is now an "evolving" global village through the influence of these disruptive technologies. Consequently, it has spurred the growth of social media in order to effectively bridge the gap. Today, social media platforms serve not only as a socializing platform but as a way to effectively sell and advertise your goods to those in the far-reaching parts of the world, and the basic tenets of achieving this goal has changed, yeah, changed drastically, that's why reading this book will really help you to gain a massive number of subscribers and needed exposure for your brand in this new year. Trust me, the sky is your limit.

## 1. Social Media as a Communication Hub

For years, social platforms like Facebook, Instagram, and YouTube have become popular as a means of sharing ideas, videos, and digital photos. People come online to connect with old friends, colleagues, distant relatives, and also meet new people across the world who share similar personal and perhaps, career interest, backgrounds, and activities. More so, it brings people together, no thanks to the rapid advancement in mobile and internet technology. An individual anywhere in the world could just post his thoughts or concerns on Facebook or Instagram, thereby drawing attention and generating comments from people with similar thoughts and interests in the comment section. Yes, it's a game changer; as it filled the silent longing in our heart for social interaction in this fast moving and busy world. This is why a movie fan could easily connect with other people around the world who share the same interest as them.

## 2. Social Media as an Entertainment Hub

Virtually everyone has some videos, photos, or ideas to share at some point or other, especially things that pique our interest. No doubt, there were limitations to the way with which you could share your videos, pictures, and ideas. However, the introduction of YouTube and Instagram changed the dynamics of entertainment. Now, people can directly upload and share their videos at no charge, and it will be viewed by others in other parts of the world. Therefore, people took it as an opportunity to showcase their talents and skills to the world, hence building followers and a fan base across the globe.

## 3. Social Media Platforms as a Means of Marketing

In the last decade, social media has gained much notoriety as a means of making income. In fact, so many digital marketers and companies alike, have built a financial empire off the bounties of digital marketing. Organizations and industries alike now choose social media, especially popular platforms like Facebook, Instagram, and YouTube for their marketing hub. According to recent research, 24% of the over six thousand global marketers who were surveyed revealed that the social media platform has been an important part of their marketing strategy for the past five years. They utilize these platforms to spread awareness and to promote their product. So, why has it become the main mode of marketing? Well, the reason is not far from the fact that it affords marketers an opportunity to tailor their content to what is likely going to resonate with its targeted audience. For instance, unlike traditional marketing channels, a diaper-producing company can easily focus their products on targeted nursing mothers or creches. In addition, it has the single advantage of appealing to a large audience at once. Besides the fact that organizations find it more convenient to reach out to new customers, it also affords them an opportunity to measure and track the success rate.

## 4. Why I wrote this book

To be frank, to get the best out of digital marketing in this year 2019, you need to stand up to the game. No longer a walk in the park. The social media world is known to change faster than any other existing online space. Things (digital marketing) are no longer what they use to be. Sadly, keeping up with it has become a Herculean task. Most especially when you are "stocked" with stale knowledge on digital marketing skills. Technology keeps evolving and you (as a digital marketer) need to keep up with the latest trend so as to grow organically and effectively reach out to your targeted audience. Gone are the days when compelling contents on Facebook, Instagram, and YouTube led to a fast-social media following, back then on YouTube, "any" video earns you a viral following; you can always be sure that your post will get to your audience

Times are changing, a well-known trend amongst digital marketers have faded away. The rules are changing, and it is vital for you to learn how to stay afloat. More so, it is important to learn how to excel in this industry. The tenets, for this reason, I have painstakingly research consumers and what makes them engage with brands. After careful research, I have been able to create a stunning list of 100 digital marketing tricks to help you excel in this niche this year 2019.

# Chapter 1: General Marketing Tricks

## 1. Set Your Objectives

Every great achievement starts at a point. Success springs out from the foundation we have laid at the beginning of our decision. The field of digital marketing is really broad and vast. Just like the saying, 'Jack of all trades, master of none', a lack of digital marketing objective can get you lost in the pool of effort. Moreover, you end up frustrated, and consequently join the pool of failed digital marketers. There is a need to understand that there is an increasing number of wannabe digital markets like you and there are professional influencers already dominating the field. Firstly, ask yourself, 'What are you going to offer that will give you an edge in the digital marketing field?' Viewers on Facebook, Instagram and YouTube are more inclined to visit content that meets their interest.

Therefore, define your overall vision and

objective. It works best if you have them written out and itemized in order of priority (write them out). The real deal is that your digital marketing must fit well into your grand plan and define your purpose. There must be a great degree of correlation between the two, otherwise, it can result in your efforts not having a real impact on your bottom-line.

Once again, ask yourself: how old is your ideal target audience? Where do they live? Africa? Europe? Rural? Are they male or female? What race or culture do you target? The better you can answer this demographic information, the faster you reach your targeted audience, and the more successful you will become in your digital marketing career. Remember, the difference between the successful and the unfulfilled digital marketers is dependent on how well the objectives are defined. Your objectives should effectively identify the problems faced by the targeted persona and offer a better solution.

## 2. Speak the Language of Your

## Audience

One common cause of failure amongst digital marketers is that they lose connection with their audience. It is easy to deviate from the desired content and deliver something different in a bid to increase your followers base, KPI settings, channel selection, and budget fretting. Tailor your content to meet the emotional needs of your target audience. Imagine targeting an advertisement of a baby care product to 70% males or teenagers on Facebook; people who really have no use of the product. The secret to successful digital marketing on social media is to satisfy the deepest desires of your target audience; create something that keeps them glued and make them keep coming back for more. For instance, an ad that will appeal to a man may not have an effect on a woman. A teen will be more inclined towards an ad campaign that will make him feel special, affirmed, or on 'top of the world'. This involves language that appeals more to their age group and draws their attention. An ad with quality and interesting images will attract the attention of a kid more than content with simple words. Unlike women, men tend to process information and decide in a linear fashion. A man doesn't need much before he decides whether to purchase a product or not. The primary message is what matters to them. "Buy this" or "shop here" is enough to drive them. The advertisement must delve deeply into their emotional goals, appeal to their inner desires, stoke their aspirations, and contain all the factors that could make them reflect on their unconscious and conscious desires. According to an online poll, people within the age range of 18 – 29 visit Instagram more than people within the age range of 50 – 64. Therefore, an advert which doesn't appeal to people within the age range of 18 – 29 is bound to have a low turnout.

## 3. Reviewing Your Marketing Strategy

Your strategy is your paddle to success in the social media world. It determines how well you stand out amongst competitors. Your marketing strategy should not be rigid. Rather, it should be subjected to constant evaluation because your initial strategy may not be perfect enough to get you the needed audience. Remember, it's a competitive world and you need to shore up. The fact that an advert is getting huge traction on Facebook doesn't mean it will have the same rate of success on YouTube. No. Each social media platform has its own group of viewers. Therefore, it is advisable to constantly check the elements that make up your digital strategy. This will enable you to quickly identify and isolate elements that are not functioning. Mind you, it could be anything, especially things that are not directly related to the cause. For instance, it could be the time of the post or the taglines of the ad. Therefore, the elements of your ad should be dependent on the KPI you've set for yourself. This will enable you as a marketer to easily evaluate the effectiveness of your campaigns on all marketing channels. With this, you can decide what steps to take to achieve your set goal. It could be to redesign the adverts or to focus more on a particular social media channel than others. Although Facebook, Instagram, YouTube, and other major platform have a large pool of viewers, it is sometimes hard to tell what advert to place in which without a careful analysis of the performance of each campaign on it. Sometimes, it's worth revising a previous analysis (if any) or trying something entirely different and creating a clearly defined KPI for it. In addition, it could be a change in target audience, putting into consideration the age group and interest or perhaps the social media network used.

## 4. Think, Review and Think Again

As much as Facebook, Instagram, and YouTube are crucial for building a fast brand following, it is good to think and strategize before posting an ad on a social media platform. Sadly, some big and small brands don't think before posting an ad. The ripple effect of such an unnoticed mistake could be devastating. In minutes, it can become a liability when something goes wrong. More so, it's difficult to take back a social media mistake. No thanks to screenshots and 4G technology for fast download. This has made the options of "delete" on most social media channels like Facebook, YouTube, and Instagram, really ineffective. Top influencers and fast-growing social media marketing brands are aware of the dangers of creating a wedge between them and their online followers. Sometimes, a well-meaning ad on Facebook could backfire. Also, an ad on Instagram could make people cringe, thus creating an effect contrary to the original intent of the poster. Contents must be thoroughly examined from a critical and unbiased lens. It is best practice to have someone else take a good look at them before posting on the social network. We all have different values, cultures, and experiences, and these define our thoughts and direction. For example, an advert that appeals to a Caucasian may catch the attention of an Asian for the wrong reason, like offending his values, beliefs, culture, or make him feel totally alienated.

## 5. Presence Makes the Difference

If I had told you that customers don't trust marketing and advertising any more, would you have believed me? No? Then, you need to wake up to 2019. Many consider the customer reviews of your ad before making a purchase choice. To them, these reviews are a high-value social proof. It determines the success rate of your advertisement. On media platforms like Facebook, potential buyers could come on the comment section and have a good look at other targeted viewers' feedback before making a purchase. Remember, for every product you offer there are a thousand competitors who offer the same product. Therefore, major reviews and comments go a long way. No doubt, a well-laid feedback gives you leverage over others.

To be on the good side, set up alerts that notify you of new comments, messages, and mentions. This allows for rapid response to audience questions, hence building consumer confidence in your advertised brand.

## 6.  Keep an Eye on Your Competitor

Yes, keep an eye on your competitor. As much as this may sound unethical to you, it is the secret of social media marketing success. Thanks to Google's benchmarking report, it is easy to compare your digital marketing growth to your competitors irrespective of their location in the world. The benchmarks selection avails you an opportunity to compare your properties against all properties with similar traffic levels in the chosen geographic location. This allows you as a marketer to gain a deeper insight into trends occurring across the chosen industry. SEMrush can also be applied to get a feel of the SEO strategy of a competitor. From here, you can derive the keywords that are driving a large volume of organic traffic to their websites. This can be achieved by creating an analysis spreadsheet of their online activities in the specified period.

## 7. **Focus Your Strength Where Your Ideal Customers Are**

The biggest challenge faced by many brands, especially new ones, is social media overwhelm. Often, you find yourself reasoning whether or not you want to utilize one or all of the social media platforms. No doubt, there are a whole lot of them; Facebook, Twitter, Instagram, Pinterest, Snapchat, and the list goes on. The fact they are free (to some extent) makes you feel as if they are a complimentary marketing outlet created to help you reach out to a good number of your targeted audience. At the end of the day, you find yourself selecting all, with the mindset that having your brand presence on every social media platform leads to a great result. Well, you are wrong. It is a death trap; directing all of your marketing strength on multiple platforms at the same time results in less impact. More so, it leads to wasted time and effort. Poor conversion of the audience becomes depressing. It is a good strategy to never bite more than you can chew - take two steps backward and consider which social media platform is best for your business. I'm referring to one that will enable you to achieve your goal of driving sales and increase awareness of your brand in your targeted community. The first thing you need to understand is the purpose of each social media platform you wish to utilize for a digital marketing campaign. For instance, if you aim to target millennials, you need to focus more on platforms like Snapchat or Instagram. Most importantly, you need to have a good understanding of your targeted audience behavior and how they will discover your brand on social media. Another good point you must bear in mind is to have a good understanding of where your audience is. For instance, if you are into fashion, Instagram and Pinterest are your best bet. This is because they are more visual compared to the rest.

## 8. Consistency is the Key to Be Outstanding

You need consistency to stay at the top of this

niche. It is a good thing to lay out your objectives, review your marketing strategy, and select social media platforms that best suit your business purpose. However, you need to be consistent in order to get your desired result. Before opening a business account on social media, ensure that your content is consistent and the handle you choose is the same across all marketing channels. Your handle, or social media username, must be the same on all social media platforms you choose. Nothing is more confusing than a brand with a different username on social media platforms - it depicts inconsistency. Your brand logo should be the same, too. In fact, upload them as your profile image on all your chosen platforms. This enables people to easily remember you. Whether offline or online, it is good practice to keep a consistent tone and disposition. If your brand is friendly and fun on Facebook, the same should go for twitter or Instagram. It should never sound like it is coming from a different brand entirely. Furthermore, do not for any reason leave your brand open to customization and interpretation. A constantly changing brand personality crumbles efforts put towards awareness and the level of customer loyalty. Develop a standard for brand consistency, vet every idea for brand consistency before publishing on your social media page. For instance, Mozilla has an online guide to assist its open source community to understand how to make use of its logos and trademarks for its Firefox browser, Mozilla, and their other products.

## 9. Avoid Cross-Posting

Never, never, ever push the same content to multiple platforms. It is a taboo in social media marketing. It is a lazy and unprofessional act. In order to get the best from your social media marketing, each social media platform needs to be utilized differently. The major challenge with achieving this is that it requires planning to determine which content should be on which platform. Have it at the back of your mind that more is not always the best choice. You really need to be thoughtful and creative when determining which post goes to which social media page. Your targeted audience are searching you out to find relevant and unique contents, they only get to notice you on platforms that compliments their social behavior while on the other hand support your business objectives. When you are strategic about the content you post on social media platforms, you will get the benefits of a better engagement in no time.

## 10. Save Time: Work with the Right Tools

In as much as it's good to maintain a good social media presence, the truth is you cannot afford to spend more time on social media platform than you need to. Save your time and money by making use of specially designed social media management tools that make work easier. Hootsuite is a good example of how a social media solution can accurately streamline your social media promotion activities and help boost your productivity. With Hootsuite, you can manage your presence across all the major social media network like Instagram, Facebook, Instagram, YouTube, and LinkedIn through a single dashboard, including keeping your eye on the conversations on all the platforms at the same time. In addition, it offers you an opportunity to plan up to 350 social media post at the same time. With one click, you can respond to news, comments, and mentions across all social media channels.

## 11. Be Inspired by Successful Brands

Irrespective of your strategy, it is best for you to have an eye on your competitor. Get inspired by them. Remember good artists copy; great artists steal. Yeah, I mean steal. However, not the kind of stealing you are thinking, like stealing the Van Gogh's infamous 'Starry Night' painting, of course not. It's more like getting inspiration from your competitors but doing it so perfectly well that everyone that gets to see it thinks it's your idea. Inspiration is the precursor of innovation. Building on the work of others has always proven to be the fastest way to get to your endpoint. George Washington said, "If I have seen further, it is because I have stood upon the shoulders of them that are before me." Never hesitate to adopt a successful strategy that has worked for other brands. You can go further by modifying them in order to get the best result. Carefully study the content of competitors within your niche; how they caption their pictures, quality of their photos, time of posting, the content of their photo, their hashtags, everything they post a significance. Figure out what you can get from their content marketing effort. Some of the questions you should get answers to are:

What are they doing as a brand to show their company's personality on social media?

How much of their content are they putting out and how are they being delivered?

What level of content are they delivering?

Are your competitors capitalizing on new or perhaps different content types?

Get a deep insight on how they built the number of their followers and replicate such. Integrate their tactics and strategy into yours. Track all their activities. The best way to do this is to be their follower too or check their business page as frequently as needed. Let them stimulate you and inspire you towards your own successful ad campaign. These feats will lift you out of the crowd.

## 12. Follow Online Conversation About Your Brand

A good way to build interest and loyalty is to provide a quick response to inquiries from both old and potential customers. There are so many brands out there that offer the same service as you, and the best way to keep the audience that shows interest in your product is to give a fast response to their inquiries. In today's society, social media platforms have. To some extent, taken the place of personal conversation, like a prospect walking into your brick and stone office to make an inquiry regarding your product.

Studies have shown that most customers, about 80 percent, expect you to respond to inquiries quickly, irrespective of the social media platform you choose to establish your presence. It is a "customer age" Therefore, a prompt response to their inquiries will make your brand appear more human to them. Remember that they are tired of being spoken to by brands; they want to have a real-time conversation with you. To have successful marketing on social media, you need to master the art of communicating with people in a manner that stimulates their emotions. Additionally, you need to speak a language that resonates with your customers, and in a way that is clear and understandable to them. Emotional attributes that are important to most customers are: Friendliness, responsiveness, helpfulness, and thoughtfulness. At the end of your interaction, your customers should have the personal feeling that your brand knows them.

## 13. Never Underestimate the Power of Life Events

Targeting the right audience with a well-strategized social media marketing campaign is a good step towards boosting your revenue. In fact, going after your audience at the right time, irrespective of their location on the globe, is an incredibly effective step. Furthermore, learn how to leverage the power of life events in order to have a great marketing campaign.

Learn to leverage the events in your audience lives to create a timely, accurate, and super relevant advert that targets people during the times of major change. Facebook is the perfect platform to perform this trick. You will have an idea of what a "life event" looks like on Facebook; it strikes a memory. Yeah, all those kinds of stuff and events that make us feel good about ourselves. They are nostalgic, to say the least. Your nemesis from high school lands your dream job, your ex-crush gets engaged to that nerd. As a social media marketer, you should be creative enough to make use of these life events as a foundation for a social media marketing campaign. People get married almost every day, a lot of babies are born into the world every day; it's all about sending the right content to them. Yes, I mean content that strikes their emotions. To make it easier for you, you can specify how soon you want your campaign ad to appear to your target audience as soon as an event take place. For instance, if you manage wedding venues, you could schedule your ad to appear to your target audience, especially newly engaged couples after 4 to 5 weeks. If you are an online baby clothing retailer, you could set your ads to appear to couples shortly after announcing that they are expecting a baby. The end game is to win the price, which to you, is more sales.

## 14. Make Use of Twitter to Test Content Ideas

Most times, if not all, the difference between a successful campaign ad and an unsuccessful one lies in content. Content that drives great engagement is not by luck nor a walk in the park. A lot of work has been put into place before it is been used. The best place to test the potentials of an idea or to gauge your targeted interest in the subject area is twitter. This is a secret most social media marketer are yet to know. Some don't bother to dive into the power to tap into hot topics that can trigger huge engagements. It is your "content lab"; your promotional tools for content marketing initiatives. For instance, as a fashion brand, you come across a concept that sounds interesting and promising. You can tweet it to gauge how well received your content is likely to be. After which you make use of twitter analytics to evaluate the performance of the tweet you tweeted from an engagement perspective. If the engagement rate is lower than needed, drop the idea and search for another. On the other hand, you can make use of them if the engagement is high.

## 15. Layer Your Target Options

Bygone are the days when social media advertisers had to content themselves with broad targeting options with their social media advertising. Today, the possibilities of specific targeting are unlimited. I mean absolutely unlimited; you can go as far as specifying age, gender, work, way of life, culture, region, educational attainment, community, the list goes on and on. More so, you will have a better result if you will master the art of layering. This involves layering the aforementioned targeting options with some additional data, such as purchasing behavior, and cultural attitude to products and the like. In addition, it involves leveraging this powerful combination to create a timely and relevant campaign. For instance, if your brand centers on pediatric medical products, you would not only leverage your target on parents between the age of 27 and 40 with at least a high school education and a household income of more than $50,000 per year, but also those with special needs kids or specific medical condition. The targeting option can easily access through an in-market segment. It is not just limited to purchasing behavior as stated in my earlier example; it could be anything, hobbies, places visited, life events, interests, or any other targeting demographics. It is a mix and match thing. Therefore, make use of this option to create a highly customized and laser-focused custom audience.

## 16. Admit When You Make a Mistake

It's tough, right? It is hard to admit a mistake, especially when it is on a public platform like social media. Some will say it's humiliating but admitting to your error is a core part of a successful digital marketing strategy. Truth be told, no matter how much effort you put into avoiding errors on your social media platform, there are high chances of committing errors, however simple it may seem. It may be your employee posting at the wrong hour or being accused of being insensitive to a consumer complaint i.e. no empathy or perhaps mixing up their personal account with business accounts. Trying to erase these errors rather than admitting to them will make your firm look worse. Whenever something goes wrong, the first thing you need to do is to acknowledge your mistake. Take good time to craft your response, rather than hastily posting a knee-jerking reaction that will cause more damage than good. Some brands go as far as deleting their account or blocking the comment section; it doesn't work that way. It is better to take an extra moment of your time to deliver a carefully worded and appropriately measured response to your band of followers. Be smart, but never try to hide your mistakes. The sin of acting like there was no mistake is unpardonable. You need to accept the responsibility of an offensive comment or a post that people deem offensive. Followers take screenshots of a post, so deleting the post doesn't make a difference. In fact, you will be surprised seeing a copy of the post you think you have gotten rid of being circulated on the internet. Neither push back nor argue with your followers that the mistake wasn't as bad as they presume. Rather, be sincere and acknowledge what transpired and you understand the fact that they are really upset with you. This shows them that your business is responsible and cares about its customers enough to empathize with their feelings.

## 17. Be Active

Here is another tip that seems really obvious, but it's so important that it's worth reiterating upon. You need to invest a good measure of your time on your social media platform. It is in your interest to ensure that you post frequently and consistently, quality and noteworthy contents, not some creepy last piece material. If you allow your brand to become lax, you will steadily lose followers and fail to attract new ones. They will fall away rapidly. Yes, this feat requires full commitment. A halfhearted commitment to your social media marketing platforms where you have a presence is the same as having zero commitment. Most times, it is worse. Your activeness enables you to humanize your brand: your converts and potential audience will feel they have some level of personal relationship with your brand. Humanizing is compulsory to ensure your brand achieves its objective of making use of social media as a marketing platform. Furthermore, being active means your brand (you or your employee) is available at most times, if not at all times. This helps you to create a strong emotional bond with your audience and prospects, hence strengthening the relationship and enabling a higher level of conversion. Alternatively, if you fail to connect with your customers (audience) on a personal level, the odds against you will increase significantly. They will lose connection with your brand. Take time to listen, respond, and engage with your audience. Remember, having a centralized plan for active engagement is a better option for your brand. Your customer is king. Since you wouldn't ignore someone that walks right to your store or calls you on the phone, you should never ignore a customer that takes the time to address you on a social platform.

## 18. Offer Customer Service

Customer service is key to the expansion of any

business. Truth be told, consumers are increasingly turning to social media for customer service. No doubt, the idea of calling or sending mail to a company's customer service center is dying away. This development is really intimidating, especially to a new business that is not yet familiar with providing online support via a social media platform. However, it is a major opportunity for your brand to prove its credibility if handled well. The fact that online customers are gradually becoming the main source of revenue for most businesses will put you at a disadvantage if you don't subscribe to it fully.

Adopting social customer service will no doubt help your marketing effort by helping to boost your company reputation. You ask me how? Since it's an open field, all the help you render on social media will automatically become visible to other visitors. Thereby demonstrating to your audience your business commitment to high-quality service. The more helpful you are, the more people will become aware of your commitment to digital platforms. Mind you, there is a need to exercise utmost caution when handling customer data online, in the cause of responding to a customer's questions and inquiry. There will be instances when you will need to move the conversation to a private section. Your customers' personal information, such as email address, phone number, or other personal details should not be displayed in the comment section.

# Chapter 2: Facebook Digital Marketing Tricks

No doubt Facebook is one of the largest social media networks, if not the largest. Virtually everyone you meet is on this platform. Its availability to people in all walks of life has given it prominence amongst all classes of people around the world. Today, the social giant which started as a place of connection with old friends and people of similar interests now boasts millions of business pages. Furthermore, it boasts of about 2 billion active users, with a greater percentage claiming to be "always online'. This has made it the perfect launch pad for ad and brand positioning. Today, Facebook houses about 80 million emerging businesses on its platform. However, it is good to note that Facebook's vast opportunity has also made it a battleground for fierce competition for prospect valuable attention and time. Virtually every organization or digital marketer has targeted this platform for its ad. To stand out from the crowd, there is a need to pay optimum attention to how you treat your presence on this platform. Before we explore the latest digital marketing tricks for this platform in 2019, you need to understand that everything you do on this platform matters, no matter how small. Often, it's the subtler quality of a digital marketer page set up or content strategy that brings about an edge in terms of ad performance on Facebook.

## 1. A Perfect Profile Picture Sounds Cool

How do you feel when you receive a friend request on Facebook from someone without a profile picture? Not interested, right? Perhaps, when someone without a personal picture on its profile sends you a message and claims to be an old friend.

In digital marketing on Facebook, your profile picture matters. Heck! It is your first impression. In other words, it is your solid ground to gain the first attention of your targeted followers. Your brand's profile picture serves as the first element potential followers will see when they engage you through a comment or via a search. On Facebook, imagery is the most important element and it's best to keep it simple. The brand picture must be stylish, as this reflects professionalism. The appropriate size for a picture on Facebook should be at least a minimum of 180*180 pixel. Compressing a large image to fit into the Facebook profile page makes it lose quality. A head shot with a standard quality close-up is good for a solo brand. However, it must be a professional looking shot, as a snapshot with some random phone ends up either blurry or dark. This may not settle well with some of your potential followers. A digital advert on sunshades may involve snapping a high-quality picture of the head of a man wearing the sun shades. Followers address you based on what we portray to them. If you display unprofessionalism, they will treat you in the same respect. So, it's best to have a good thought before putting in a picture on your ad page. Firstly, it must rhyme with your brand and also it must show quality. At first look, a potential follower should be able to tell who you are and what you offer. As a firm, it is best to have a simple company logo with a moderate vibe; it should reflect clarity. When a brand logo is simple and moderate in design, your potential follower's mind is able to process it quickly and efficiently. An example of this is the HubSpot logo.

## 2. Make Your Cover Photo Worth the Second Look

Before designing a cover photo, you must first realize that your Facebook account is an extension of your business. It tells a lot about you and your brand. A Facebook cover photo is designed to take a significant chunk of your Facebook page, it is your Facebook banner and the most noticeable part of your page. When viewed on most desktop browsers, it takes up to a quarter of the screen. It is really important as it creates a first impression (just like your profile picture). A cover photo can be compared to what you are wearing to work. You wouldn't wear a T-shirt and a pair of jeans for a professional business meeting or to meet a new client, right? You wouldn't dare. It will really create a bad impression. So, your cover photo is as important as your profile picture; it reflects your passion and level of professionalism. Your cover photo sets the tone for everything on the page. Although the use of text on a cover photo is okay, as long as it tallies with the brand, it is best to keep them concise. A cover photo with text above 20% will confuse the visitor. He will end up clicking off the page. It could be two-three statements; "Onward Together", "Grow Better", "Think Big", "Nothing is impossible". It must be informative and engaging i.e. appeal to the emotion of your targeted potential follower. What appeals to youth might be a huge turn off to a teenager. Your cover photo should contain a brand slogan that will move your targeted audience to action. In addition to this, it must include a centerpiece to focus a potential follower's attention, tagged along with a color scheme that matches the brand tone. Today, there are standard digital marketing tools which can help you design a professional looking cover page. A typical example of this is Landscape; this tool can help you design a perfect brand cover in a few minutes.

## 3. A Video will do the Trick Better

Yes, I mean a video on your business page. Isn't it amazing? A video length of 20 to 90 offers you as a social media marketer an amazing opportunity to be more creative and engaging. Videos make an excellent storyteller. A video generates about 1200% more likes and shares than a picture. It receives the most engagement. Truth be told, it is the most perfect cocktail to boost your conversion. No wonder most of the ads on Facebook news feed are usually videos. Facebook records over 8 billion video views per day. Yes, 8 billion views from over 2 billion active users. Video brings in two major things that naturally catches human attention: Noise and movement makes it an undisputable attention grabber on Facebook and other social media platforms. Studies have shown that an average viewer remembers about 95% of a message conveyed when it is watched compared to when read. They make conveyed information more digestible to the human mind.

Facebook users spend over a hundred million hours a day watching video on Facebook. A video on your Facebook business page can include music, text, photographs, or links. The key thing about it is to keep it simple and understandable to the targeted audience. If well utilized it is a perfect trick for increasing fan base and also encouraging existing fans to spend more of their valuable time engaging with your brand. This helps in improving prospecting and engagement. However, it must be eye-catching and entertaining enough to stop the targeted audience in their tracks. In a bid to build more followers, it is best to start incorporating high-quality video content in your feed.

## 4. Understand the Magic of Facebook Algorithm

Have you ever wondered why some posts receive a crazy amount of engagement and comment while others just fall flat a few minutes after being posted? Sometimes, it reeks of some form of favoritism; some gain huge traction while others are just there. Calm down; it is not magic. It is the work of the Facebook Algorithm. It is responsible for ranking all potential posts that can display on a user news feed. This is dependent on how likely the viewer will react positively with the displayed content in its news feed. The Facebook algorithm is made up of four key components to rank what appears first on the customer feed: Inventory, Signals, Predictions, and Overall Score. These four contents work together to give your targeted customer the best experience on their social platform. The signal stage is where many digital marketers on Facebook lose it. It is where your content is being examined. A low-quality ad picture will surely have a poor score in this section. You can't snap a picture with a random android phone with some mobile application editing and expect to be ranked well. No, it doesn't work that way: the margin between a successful ad and an unyielding one is value. Yes, value. A step forward (in value) leads to success on Facebook and vice versa. Do I need to remind you that there are millions of ads posted on Facebook every day, with many offerings just virtually the same thing you offer and targeting your potential followers? Your content should show class and professionalism. This gives you a 95% chance of your content being seen in the news feed of a large number of potential followers. As a beginner, there is a need to avoid gearing your strength towards posting self-promotional content; it will do you no good. Yes, Facebook prefers a content post that makes a user stay within its wall. It will rank you lower than those posts that encourage users to remain active on its platform. Your best bet in drumming up new followers and riling up your current ones is to build up content that will rank well.

## 5. Be the Master of Facebook Algorithm

The power to determine whether your ad post will ever get to the news feed of your targeted audience is in your hands. You heard me right, in your hands. It's all about out-beating Facebook algorithm. When creating an ad post, you need to ask yourself a vital question: what type of interaction do you want to generate? Rather than focusing on building content that will drive popularity or grab the attention of your audience. It is better to gear your effort towards what makes your ad conversation-worthy. A post to drive active interaction will rank more on Facebook algorithm than a post that will drive a passive one. Your page post must be able to drive comments, shares, and reaction. This is the three secrets you must have at the back of your mind to be a successful Facebook marketer. A passive action only drives random clicking and viewing while an active page post that has the potentials to drive conversation between viewers will show higher on the news feed of targeted audience. However, in achieving this feat there is a need to avoid using engagement bait. Stop goading people into commenting. For example, comment "yes" if you want a free copy, let us have your view. It will do you more harm than good. Furthermore, it will result in the demotion of your post on your audience news feed. Facebook also places importance on sharing, unlike the days when the chances of your post been higher on your targeted audience news feeds are dependent on the number of times your brand post has been shared. Today, Facebook algorithm favors shared posts that sparks conversations amongst families and friends. For instance, if an existing follower shares a post from your brand's Facebook page, and his friends and families start to comment on the shared post, then the post will continue to appear to other people. In the other way around, if a share from your business page doesn't generate comments, the post will be demoted in the Newsfeed. Apart from comment, the reaction is another determinant of how well your brand post will reach your targeted audience within the news feed. Of course, not everyone will comment or share your brand post on Facebook. Reaction helps Facebook algorithm to determine the quality of your content, as quality is the most crucial piece for moving forward.

## 6. Ascend the Ladder of Diversification

Diversifying your content distribution is the best and latest marketing trick to make your brand page post to show up on your followers feed. Don't just place an ad and hope for the best out of it. Diversify and test different types of ads: Video ads, Customer testimonials, product carousels, etc. Today, Facebook offers digital marketers an opportunity to be creative, there exists more diverse and types for business than before. Apart from Video ads, the platform now boasts Carousel ads, slide show ads, Collection ads, Dynamic ads, Link ads, Lead ads. A carousel ad offers a digital marketer an avenue to offer multiple images of offers in one go. This offers your targeted audience a richer and better experience. A Link ad has the power to encourage action and to increase conversion through its customizable CTA button to direct targeted prospects to a landing page. Understanding the uniqueness of each ad type is a key factor to a successful brand post. Moreover, the larger the amount of quality and relevant ad content you post, the greater your chances of appearing on your target news feed. Each ad post should feed each other, they should complement each other.

## 7. Be Granular About Your Persona

Don't be specific; be extremely specific. If I had told you that on Facebook, it is possible to narrow your brand ads towards French and English-speaking men between the age of 18 – 33, who live in a 14-mile radius mile in Boston. Would you have believed? I guess your answer is a no. Over the years, Facebook has done a lot to make digital marketing more and more personal. As much as this can be sometimes be annoying to shoppers, it is a sure-fire way to attract shoppers. This is because they are seeing brand ads that they are genuinely interested in. Facebook offers businesses on its platform an opportunity to layer their targeting options upon each other. This unequal sophisticated level of target ad makes Facebook marketing an exciting and reliable venture. However, if you are too specific in your targeting, it really could work against you. You might end up meeting some potential customer who might be needing the brand you are advertising. It is best practice to dedicate your time to analyze your targeted customer base and analyze their personas. For instance, if your brand product is a business tool, e.g. a laptop, then a rural community should not be in your buyer's persona. It is a dead end. In developing a buyer persona, you need to consider the characteristics of your targeted audience, their behaviors, their objectives, and the demographic data. Demographic data helps you to segment your targeted audience into a well-refined sub-category. It involves deciding the age, gender, level of education. In deciding your targeted consumer behavior, you might need to employ the help of analytics tools to measure behaviors as the conversion path of your targeted audience and potential paths to their conversion. Then, you can use your designed personas to go after potential consumers of your brand or offerings.

## 8. How About Timing

Besides putting good effort into creating good content for your Facebook business page, it is essential to watch out for the best time to post it. On Facebook, timing is the key; it is everything. Good content posted at a wrong time might not generate an impact. Your post must coincide with the time your targeted followers are likely to be most active. Imagine posting an ad targeted toward teens at a late hour of the night or at hours they are likely to be in school. It's a dead end. Optimizing your post timing doesn't necessarily mean posting in real-time. It could be the early hours of the morning or afternoon as the case may be. Posting a brand ad in the early afternoon during weekdays is ideal for most brands, most especially brands that target audience between the age range of 18 – 44. According to Co-schedule, if a great percentage of your targeted audience is in the United States, then the best time to post is the Eastern time zone. If your targeted audience is in other parts of the world, first of all, determine their geographical location, compare their time zone in relation to yours and post at their peak hours. On weekends post your brand ad between 12 – 1pm, on Thursdays and Fridays, post your brand ad between 1 pm – 4pm. On Wednesdays post between 3 – 4pm. According to the schedule, people tend to be in good moods on Fridays. There are chances that if your brand post falls into this, happy index, there are chances of a higher engagement rate than other days of the week.

To ease out the stress of manual posting at peak hours, Facebook offers business page social scheduling options. This option allows you to set up your Facebook to automatically push your brand post during peak engagement hour. Isn't that cool? It ensures your targeted audience does not miss your post. Your post only comes up when your targeted active users are online. This takes a huge weight off your shoulder, it abolishes the stress and anxiety associated with manual posting. Manual posting is not fun, you burn out with time. With scheduling options on Facebook, you no longer need to calculate time zones for your targeted audience. Facebook does that for you. Furthermore, it gives you a ton of time to engage other positive activity. You can use the extra time to make new connections and perhaps get into an important conversation. Truth be told, if you really want to have an effective Facebook presence, scheduling your post in advance is a must do for you.

## 9. Post Frequently

Yes, posting more content increases your chances of visibility. According to buffer, there is a 24% increase in the volume of post per quota. Brands with a business page on Facebook have begun to increase their posts per day. Posting more content increases your chances of been seen. In fact, Facebook encourages brands to post frequently on their pages. Bygone are the days when there was a need to worry about the risk of flooding your followers and target audience with your content, hence turning them off. There is no need to have such worries again, as there are fewer chances of the same user seeing all your posted content. Newsfeed shows each of your targeted audience the most relevant story, this makes it the chances of the same person seeing all your post really low. It is estimated that pages that post on average of 5 times daily receive up to 2,465 engagement per post; totaling 12,330 while those who post above 10 receive an average of 1,202 engagement per post, a total of 12,020. Therefore, posting up to 5 times per day should be your target. However, it is important to note that the quality and value of your content must not be sacrificed for this feat, or else your targeted audience will lose interest and click you off. Your post must maintain the ability to engage your audience. It is what makes them keep coming and sharing. Post your brand ad as often as you have useful and engaging content to share.

## 10. Have You Tapped the Potential of "About Us"?

You would be surprised that your "About Us" page is as powerful as your content post. How often have you found yourself going to check the "About Us" page of brands whose ads piqued your interest on Facebook? Well, I have done that a million times. It is called a fact-finding mission. You'd be surprised that the "about us" page of most businesses on Facebook are next to barren or filled with scanty information. Although the interest of visitors vary, most people, however, are concerned about an elementary piece of information that defines you: who you are, your location, what you do, how you do it, when you started, what's in it for them, and how you came to be where you are today. The "about us" page should be goal-oriented, it should highlight the most convincing selling points of your story and brand, satisfying the curiosity of your potential audience. Your about page is the best place to boost the confidence of you of your visitors. To prove to them that you have the skills, the experience they need and your brand is the best among the rest. You aren't the only one offering the product or services. They need to solve their problem, all they need is an assurance that your product or service is capable to meet their needs flawlessly. A good formula to create a convincing About Us page is: Firstly, set the scene, introduce the problem, rise to the challenge, arrive at a solution and envision what is next. It is important to ensure that all your business information is clearly stated on the about us page. This should include your website, social links, and contact information.

## 11. Your Response Time Shows Us How Serious You Are

Sometimes the secret to standing out amidst a vast number of competitors is to provide the best customer care. It is irreplaceable. Response time is the gap between gaining a potential customer and losing one for good. A step in either direction will have a lasting impact on the success of your brand ad on Facebook. People always have concerns and question to ask, especially when it is a new product been released. They usually have a high level of expectations from brands, in terms of timing and accuracy of their response to the question asked. It is unethical to let your target audience comments rally for too long before you respond to them. It is estimated that, on social media, an average follower expects a brand to respond to their inquiry within a space of four hours. It is best practice to make a conscious effort to respond to notifications in no-time. Sometimes, this can be really tricky, most especially when you publish an ad through Facebook's power editor and never see it again. This sometimes makes many of your potential customer's inquiry unattended to. Do I need to remind you that the value of your ad is dependent on the reviews and comment on your followers and targeted audience make on it? Unattended ads plummet the value of your post. Your audience and other targeted followers will look for alternatives. To address this, it is best to set an alert that notifies you whenever a new comment is posted on your Brand ad. A quick response to followers' inquiry makes them trust you more, hence sharing every content that comes from you, knowing fully well that it is reliable. Potential followers who visit your brand post will be intrigued by your engagement. Furthermore, it shows them that you value their time and care about their satisfaction. Spout smart inbox offers you an opportunity to quickly respond to questions and comments in no time. Ensure your social marketing team has a bird's eye view of all the content you promote on your social media. More so, the whole team should have full access to the alerts and notifications that are coming through. However, if you lack the resources to respond to all messages, you can employ Facebook Messenger chatbot to speed up the process of your response to your targeted audience irrespective of their location on the globe

## 12. Up Engagement with a Simple Contest

The spirit to engage in competition is alive and well in all walks of life. It has its way of prompting customers to talk about your Brand. At one point or the other, you must have come across a Facebook contest ad on your news feed. It is another way to increase your brand ad engagement on Facebook. People love challenges; something to keep their mind engaged, especially when there is an incentive attached to the contest. As a Facebook marketer, you can harness this opportunity to increase customer engagement However, it doesn't have to be complicated or hard. Otherwise, it will be a turn off to some of your potential audience. it is best to keep it simple and fun induced. Yes, I mean a fun contest. Make it something people would love to engage with online. It could be a random question about your brand product, fill in the gap, a social or national event (that relates to your brand), Hashtags, cute pictures of dogs or new recipes. According to Buzzsumo, quiz contests are one of the best ways to keep your audience engaged. They discovered that a contest quiz gets shared on average of 1900 times. It's all about creativity. You can even tell them to submit a picture of them using your product, make a comment on your product and then you choose the winner for a fun trip or send them an exclusive brand of yours. For instance, there was a time when Harpoon brewery asked people to share what their love life means to them, after which there would be a random selection for the winner to attend Harpoon Fest. Isn't that an enticing incentive? Tell me, which beer lover wouldn't want a free visit to the best beer-fests in Boston? Running a contest with an enticing incentive is the best way to spur activity on Facebook. To make it really official, your contest could be live on your brand website where an interested contestant can search for it; then use Facebook to promote the official site. However, when conducting a contest on Facebook, have it in the back of your mind that there are some promotions that Facebook does not allow. Some of them are: Asking your followers and fans to like your brand page as a criteria to participate in the contest, Asking your followers to upload your brand cover picture or any picture promoting your brand as their own in order to participate, telling your fans to tag their friends and families as part of the contest, and asking your followers to share the contest on their timeline in order to enter the contest. Furthermore, there should be some form of clarity in terms of eligibility, requirement, and how the winner will be selected.

## 13. Be Bizarre

Does that sound strange? Yes, post something that will catch the attention of your target audience. Be an unconventional marketer; it could be a picture of anything, not talking about horrible things like a picture of a lion eating a deer, or a cheetah chasing its prey. It should be something that will strike the happy part of the emotion of your target audience. Facebook viewers love funny pictures. Therefore, it could be the picture of a toddler acting like an adult, a picture of a dog acting like a human, or a cat doing crazy stunts. Who doesn't love babies or dogs? Even if they don't seem related to your brand, you can make them related to it by adding funny brand related captions. The picture must rhyme with the caption. Mind you, don't just post funny pictures on your pages without an appropriate caption or a sound reason behind it. It might create a negative effect. Remember, the goal is to gain the attention of your audience and potential consumers of your brand. People come online with a "relaxed" mindset. Being too serious as a Facebook marketer is not a good idea. Your target audience might end up clicking you off, not because they are not interested but probably because of their current mood or situation. A little playfulness will do the trick. It will grab the attention of busy, distractible, and "hurry" minded people. However, there is a need to apply moderation. For instance, if your brand is a medical product and you post nothing but dog and cat pics all the time, people will begin to doubt your authority. Some might even go as far as unliking your page.

## 14. Don't Forget Your Leads

You will know the importance of a lead to the growth of your brand. It is non-negotiable., thanks to Facebook custom audiences. Today, it is possible to upload emails on Facebook and then show your brand ad to the timeline of the owners of the email address. Gather the email address of the leads you have acquired via newsletter sign up, lead generation companies, or perhaps that of your current customer you wish to upsell to or export your email as a CSV from Hubspot, market, or whatever CRM you use. You can craft your brand ad you intend sending to your contacts in a personalized way. This makes them feel connected to you. For instance, let's assume you have a list of people who downloaded a .pdf file on how to build a blog, you can load their email address on Facebook custom audience and push a highly specific and personal Ad that tells them what next step they need to take their blog to the next level or how they can monetize their blog. This will increase the chances of them responding to your ad. As a producer of a consumable product such as cookies, Candies, snickers, you can use this medium to push advertisements of your new product to your potential audience.

## 15. Mirror Your Audience

With time, after gaining a good number of audiences for your brand on Facebook, you can clone them. Facebook allows for that, it offers you an opportunity to clone your Facebook audience, hence expanding your reach. This helps address the challenges of not having emails or phone numbers of potentials leads for conversion. Through Facebook's lookalike audience features, it is possible to expand an existing audience by finding new leads that possess the same attributes as your performing audience. It's that simple. It matches your followers' list with their millions of data points to generate a detailed picture of an ideal audience. Facebook offers you an opportunity to choose the range of 1% - 10% of the population of your targeted country. You can use this feature to clone your top performing audience. They will be a reflection of your ideal target but are not yet on the list of your followers. If your top performing customers fall into the age of 14 – 30, have an athletic body, Caucasians, live in the urban areas, Facebook lookalike audience features will aid you to find those who possess these same features. Hence, it increases your leads. If you can tap this opportunity offered by Facebook's lookalike audience feature with targeted or personalize, you will have greater success in reaching out to a potential audience. In addition, it's best to select a lesser range of your targeted population in order to get optimum results. Selecting 1% to target yields more potential buyers than when the range is 5% or 10%. The smaller the range of the targeted population the better the result.

However, if you do not have a large number of followers on Facebook, you can still go ahead to create a lookalike audience using a tracking pixel to generate a website custom audience to mirror.

## 16. Use Emoji in Your Facebook Marketing

Do you want to gain more feedback? Then, start using emojis in every ad you post on your page. Yeah, it kind of looks dumb, right? But it actually works. According to Mark Irvine, ads with emojis tend to get a far higher rate of views than ads that do not. People tend to connect easily with emojis because it has a way of enticing them to click. They are fun. Their colors pop out in a monotonous news feed, hence drawing the attention of the target audience. Facebook offers marketers 8 categories of emoji to use for their post: Smiley & people emojis, animal and nature emojis, food and drink emojis, activity emojis, travel and places emojis, object emojis, symbol emojis, and flag emojis. Ads with emojis on Facebook usually have a 241% click-through rate than an ad without an emoji. They tend to get far more reach, viral impression, and organic impression than posts without emojis. You can make use of this trick to increase your click-through rate. However, using Facebook emojis inappropriately exposes you to the risk of alienating both your customer and you. Careful consideration needs to make in regards to your existing and potential customer base. How will you feel when you see a law firm in your news feed making use of an emoji? Strange, right? It may fly for Daycares, entertainment companies, food companies, and the like. If your service or brand is typically consumed by a young audience, millennials, and moms, then it makes sense for you to use emoji freely. If your target audience happens to be middle-aged men or senior citizens, there is a high probability that your post will be met with confusion.

## 17. Increase Your Transparency

Increasing the level of transparency of your post on your page is an important trick in engaging both existing potential audiences. Especially in times like this when fake ad impressions are on the rise, consumers are becoming wary of online claims. By increasing the level of transparency of your post, you will develop and strengthen your relationship with the target audience. With Facebook, you can connect with those who love your brand. People want to get to know you, your story, what motivated you toward going into business, and why they should patronize you. You need to give them an open and inside look. As a Facebook marketer, there's a need to consider how you will interact with your audience - taking more of a social and human approach. If something goes wrong, it is best to admit to your mistakes and provide a more honest and human response to all queries on your business page. You will be surprised at the level of loyalty your audience will commit towards your brand.

## 18. Promote Your Page with Facebook Ad

Have you considered making use of Facebook ad

to promote your page? Trust me, it works like fire! According to an eMarketer survey, 96% of social media marketers concluded that Facebook is the best platform for return on investment. A Facebook ad is more targeted than you can ever imagine. With a few dollars, you can reach your targeted audience easier and faster irrespective of their location in the world. In addition, you can target users based on location, age, gender, demographics, interest, behavior, job titles, connections, and income level. It amplifies the reach of your content. Besides the fact that Facebook ads are relatively cheap compared to other social platforms, it also provides you with the opportunity to accurately sales or leads. Lastly, it helps you to frequently capture qualified leads and get more sales.

## 19. Facebook Live

Here's a trick that can definitely boost your awareness and consequently your cash flow. Believe it or not, you can now have real-time interaction with your audience on this platform.

There was a time this offer was limited to big corporations, and this gave them an unfair advantage over small business owners. With just a simple click of a button, you can effectively broadcast a live event to your followers and fans. So far, it is the most sociable way to communicate important messages to your audience. According to Facebook, its users spend more time watching videos when it is live than when it is a pre-recorded or a saved video. In fact, it's a more humane way of building your demographic base; since it's unedited and real to them. Your users can always catch up with you without missing anything. Furthermore, its built-in notification allows your followers to know when your page is 'going live'.

Want to know more?

The platform also allows users to set a reminder, so they don't forget to tune in when you are 'live'. This amazing functionality allows you as a brand to expand your reach and exposure, and it is ideal for celebrations or pre-meditated events and functions. The Facebook live interface displays your audience remarks on the live post in real time. One great thing about live videos on Facebook is that it retains your live broadcast on your page. I.e. even if your biggest fan missed the live stream, they can always come on your page to play the broadcast. Furthermore, Facebook lets you have an insight video stat and live analytically. This development lets you know the peak live viewers figures of your broadcast, your total reach, the reaction of your viewers, shares, and their comments. Moreover, it is free.

## 20. Seize the Opportunity of Vanity URL

Facebook has made it possible for your friends and fans to easily recall your profile page without going through the hassle of using the search engine. It is called vanity URL. This feature is an easy to share and easy-to-find URL that helps to drive traffic through the reinforcement of your brand. Once the number of likes you have on Facebook is up to 25, you can always request for a Facebook vanity URL. Every time a Facebook user is directed to your brand page on Facebook, your brand is automatically reinforced. It makes it really easy for Facebook users and potential followers to visit your page by typing in your brand name. An example of a Vanity URL is "facebook.com/your brand or business name". No doubt, it is easier to promote your business page via this strategy. You can easily give out a business card containing your URL page to friends, families, relatives, or perhaps individuals you met briefly, probably on public transport or at an airport, who you feel are potential clients or followers.

## 21. Rubbing on (doubling down) Your Past Success

Do you remember that ad content you randomly posted on Facebook some time back that you still bragged about? Yes, because the result was awesome You were really amazed by the flood of answers and likes. It's not luck, it is creativity. Truth be told, figuring out a creative ad content to post could be a Herculean task. The main essence of a digital marketing campaign revolves around making your followers come back for more. No doubt, it's not easy, but you may achieve a measure of success in it. So, how about reposting those updates? At this point, you probably think it's cheating. Well, it's not. In fact, it is one secret, Facebook marketers are yet to realize. Reposting and recycling previous brand ads that have brought success is another marketing tip that has been underutilized by Facebook marketers. Contents that received lots of engagement some years back will still trigger a similar reaction when posted again. However, ensure a time frame of about 3 to 6 months before posting this same ad content. This will prevent your audience from hitting you up saying, "You posted that some days back". To get an optimal result, ensure you calculate the engagement rate of the content you are reposting, as it is a reflection of the quality of your content.

## 22. Include a CTA (Call to Action)

I will tell you this: it's not rocket science to know what your target audience wants on Facebook. It's all about how unconventional you are in your bid to engage them. Remember you aren't the only brand seeking their attention on Facebook; there are a thousand and one with the same purpose. People see ad contents on their newsfeed times without number, and they will only view the ones that pique their curiosity. Unlike google ad words, which enable you to show your ad to people who are interested in buying your products at that moment, the case is so much different for Facebook marketing. With Facebook, you can never tell what your target audience is thinking when they are online. This is the reason why Facebook find out their posts receive little to no reaction. The secret of Facebook marketing is to give them something that will pique their interest; something that will give them value.

How about a Call-To-Action? Why not let them

know what you want from them? Use CTAs such as: "Share this if you know someone needs this", "click on this Ad to meet singles around you", "let's have your thoughts", "like this post if you agree". These CTAs push your followers to engage with you. More so, it increases your chances of meeting up with a potential audience. It could be in the form of a question. "Want him to notice you?", "Need to buy a Birthday gift?" "Do you want a copy". Always keep your CTA short and prominent. As a marketer on Facebook, never forget the power of the word "free". Nothing moves people on Facebook more than the word "free". Funny right? The easiest way to get your target audience to click on your Facebook ad is to offer them something of value at no cost. Imagine you as a marketer seeing ad offering you a resource on SEO at no charge, how would you react to the ad? You will find yourself clicking the ad to have access to the free resource you are been offered at no cost.

## 23. Promote Your Business Page in Your Official Email Signature

How many emails do you send out in a week? 20? 40? 100? That's a lot of potential audience to build on. Combining your Facebook links with your email signature will definitely get you tons of new fans without hassle. It is cool for credibility and brand awareness. It will help you gather some "likes", boost your customers/audience loyalty, and increase your social traffic. Truth be told, it is a great opportunity to expand your network, widen your total audience reach, increase the size of your interaction with your brand market, your brand, and increase your sales and followers. People learn more about your name, your brand and what you do. If your communication with a potential customer used to be by email alone, adding your Facebook link creates a new and better opportunity for them to connect to your business. A research study has proven that people are more likely to engage with your brand on social media (Facebook) if they have an existing connection with you. This makes Facebook an avenue for nurturing leads. You must be surprised at the number of people who will click on your Facebook link attached to your email signature. You can also use your email signature to keep your audience up-to-date on what you are doing with dynamic content such as the recent post on your Facebook business page. Facebook comments on your email signature reminds your readers of your brand quality and why they are associated with your business in the first place.

## 24. Apply the 70-20-10 Rule

This rule is the most effective way to strike a balance on content to post on your Facebook page. At one point in time or another we find our self-stuck on what to post on our Facebook page to engage our followers and not bore them away. If you have found yourself in this position before you will agree with me that it is a difficult situation. You wouldn't want to stick to one type of content; it's a dead end. Your content must be engaging, something your audience will love. Apply the 70-20-19 rule to keep your target audience engaged. Post engaging and valuable content 70% of the time, post content relevant to the interest of your followers 20% of the time. Then feel free to post self-promotional content 10% of the time. The secret is keeping it varied. Be creative. Be dynamic. Be forward thinking. You can mix up the aforementioned content rules with questions, observations about your brand and call outs. It works. A good Facebook strategy goes beyond just posting links to your official website and ad content. If you want real engagement, ask for it. How about asking a question? a poll? Something funny, that strikes their emotion. You must have found yourself visiting a business page, not because of the brand ad you saw two weeks back but because of the content that struck your happiness core, and made you feel happy. This way you end up seeing other ads the firm is pushing out.

## 25. Share User-generated Content

Do you want to increase engagement? Have you thought about toning down your own content and sharing your user-generated content? It not just saves you time and energy of coming up with an engaging post but also increases the loyalty of your fans and makes them feel included. It is the secret to receiving the most engagement on Facebook. Do your research. Successful Facebook campaigns are usually structured with user generated content. Fans enjoy creating content that incorporates the brand they really love. It is a norm for them. You can make them feel included by having them share content they have created for you or perhaps pictures of their interaction with your brand. Buffer is one organization that has really made use of this trick to increase the level of their customer engagement and it worked for them in terms of growth of their fan page. Everyone wants to feel known on Facebook, especially when they are recognized by their brand. How will you feel when you see people reposting your content about them? Or you wake up one morning and see the number of likes you have garnered as a result of the sharing of your post by your favorite brand. How will you feel? Happy right? Allowing users to be part of your business page in a personal way can help boost their bond with your brand. It works unequal wonders in driving conversions. You can host sponsored events like concerts and festivals or organize a meet and greet, depending on the size of your company. Sharing user-generated content is really a way to stand out in the crowd of businesses on Facebook

## 26. Optimize the Use of CTA Button

Have you heard the word small but mighty before? A little insignificant thing doing the works beyond its reach. That's how powerful the small CTA button you see on a brand ad on your new post can do. Never underestimate the power of the call to action. The CTA button helps you to bring the most essential objective of your business to the forefront of your Facebook page.

It helps to establish a connection between your Facebook page and sites that host your important information. Like I wrote earlier on, users will not act unless they are prompted to act, hence a post with a thumbnail that refers them to your official site or something you feel will convert them will do the trick. Facebook CTA button include contact us, book now, sign up, Shop now, play now, use App and, watch the video. It is best to ensure it lands them in a page that fulfills your conversion goals. It could be to a video that promotes your brand, an opt-in page, contact form. Once your audience clicks on the Call-To-Action button, it automatically redirects them to your other pages. This saves you the stress of posting links. However, your post must tally with the call to action. For instance, as a firm that does hospitality or restaurant business, you can use a CTA that shows them to book now, this will take them to your page where they can easily book an appointment. However, if you are a sales firm with an online presence you can always use the shop now CTA button. This will massively drive

Facebook users to your business page. It's all about using the right button.

## 27. Facebook Insight

Evaluating the success of your previous post in engaging your customer helps you determine what next step you need to take to increase your objective. Posting creative content on your business page doesn't mean you have won the battle; sometimes creative content on your Facebook page can really get you busy but not effective, that's the reason why reviewing Facebook audience insight to determine what really produce the result you are seeking. You don't just want your content to be relevant to them, you want your created content to engage them and generate some follows or likes and lead to a conversion of your targeted audience. The trick is, the more you know about your user the easier and better you can effectively target them with your ad content. This is because it is tailored to their preference. With Facebook analytics, your contents yield more results, whether it is a campaign ad or a daily business post. You ask me how? With Facebook analytics, you can measure the total number of likes on your page, including the new ones, the number of unique people who engage with your page, or each post and your post reach. With audience insight you can even expand your reach, you can test new waters within your existing audience, and find more trending topics or related interest that helps scale your online campaign. Depending on what online campaign you choose to run, the Facebook analytic tool offers you an opportunity to determine the extent of the audience you want to analyze. Is it people on your page or everyone on Facebook, or perhaps you have a selected custom audience you feel will help you increase the level of your engagement? By custom audience I mean based analysis based on age, demographics, device, interest, or gender. The secret here is the more the refined the parameter you use to define your selection of audience, the more successful you will become in advertising

## 28. Your Ad Determines the Deal

Your offer determines whether your ad will pay off or not. A dead-end offer will yield a dead-end result. Taking a swing at the new ad campaign, testing tons of interest and demographics, using a lot of high-quality images without a shot at what you offer, you won't make anything out of your ad. Forget about the 50% or the 10% discount, I am not disputing the fact that they are great ways of increasing sales of your brand, I am saying on Facebook they don't really strike the emotional part of your target audience. Imagine you are faced with the choice of choosing between an ad of some hoodies offered at 60% discount and an ad of an offer of some shirts saying purchase will feed seven dogs. Which will you go for? The first? Of course not. You will choose the second, especially if you happen to be a dog lover. You won't even consider the fact that you are purchasing a shirt. Your mind will be fixed on the seven dogs you are feeding. Get it? Great offers sell without selling. As a Facebook marketer, you must find a way to sweeten your offer. I am not talking about manipulation or hiding vital details. I am saying offer your product in a way people won't feel you are selling them something. In Brian Clark's own words "Great copy doesn't seem like an ad, it appears like a favor." As a Facebook marketer, you must have it in your mind that people don't like been sold to, but they love purchasing stuff. So, think outside the box, forget the conventional ad you see everywhere; "Free shipping on offers over $200", "Free delivery on all purchase", "30% discount on all purchase", bury them all. Your mission is to make them have the notion that whatever they purchase from you is their own idea, not yours

## 29. Be Smart

Forget the metrics and focus on sales. You didn't open a Facebook business page to garner likes and followers, you joined to increase sales of your brand by expanding your reach. You wouldn't want a thousand followers on your page and yet still make 10% sales on your product. What is the use of the likes and shares of your ad without an increase in the money you make? Despite the time spent creating engaging content and money spent on an ad campaign. On Facebook, it is easy to get drowned in the, "I just need to be patient, people are engaging my content, I will soon see the sales coming." It's a wasteful thought. Most times they never materialize. A thousand likes and shares is not a thousand sales. Although it is important, to some extent, they are. But pinpoint the ads that leads to conversion and those that don't. According to Jon Loomer, the chief founder of power hitter club, a community for Advanced Facebook marketers said, "if you as a Facebook marketer do not use conversion tracking, you will never be able to determine which AD leads to revenue or not." This leads to wrong decisions when managing ads on your Facebook page. Remember, it's sales first, CLICK and SHARE second

## 30. Amplify Your Brand with Hashtag

Have you considered using a hashtag to expand your reach to the Facebook audience who are viewing the post in your topic? I guess you must have at one time or other clicked on a hashtag on Facebook. What happened? I believe it took you to a feed a of public post. Right? Adding # to your words on Facebook is the easiest way to link with people who are interested in your niche topics. Hashtags make your post searchable on Facebook. What if I tell that on average Facebook receives a billion searches per day? Categorizing your content with a hashtag makes you a shining star in a dark sky. For instance, the #walkingDead links people who are interested in the show. Branding your Facebook business page with your own special hashtag will get you in front of people who may not have seen your post before, especially when it is a new brand. By branding all your Facebook ad posts about your new product, you can easily break the information out into a separate stream of information. This gives people an easier way to share information about your brand. An example of this is the #crashTestBeauties brand campaign. The brand tacks the tag on all their beauty testing video for particular brands, this makes someone who is totally alien to the campaign can catch on by clicking on the hashtag which leads directly to previous videos. However, there is a need to consider what other people would be interested in sharing before 'hashtaging'. A post that is more promotional than valuable may discourage people from sharing with their friends. Also, keeping your hashtag specific to your industry is really important, otherwise your updates will get lost in the fold.

## 31. Encourage Reviews on Your Ad Post

A positive customer review will bring you what others will bring to our doorstep what other marketing efforts cannot. A market research study has proven that about 88% of people, your own potential customers read reviews before deciding on the quality of a new brand, they place much trust on online reviews as they would have if it were to be a personal recommendation. It proves to the potential consumer the authenticity of the brand you offer. Consumers are more concerned about online reviews than discount offers. Reviews have the power to make or break your brand. A bad review makes customer shy away from purchasing your brand, they see the flaws, shortcomings, and how your brand cannot satisfy their needs. Encouraging your fans to write an honest review of their experience using your brand post in the comment section of your brand ad post makes a lot of difference. It helps to boost their loyalty towards your brand. Facebook offers an opportunity to rate and add pictures to their post in regards to their experience using your brand. At a glance, a user can predict whether they want to opt for your brand or look for an alternative.

# Chapter 3: YouTube Digital Marketing Tricks

Do you want to get your brand in front of many people? Try YouTube. YouTube has the power to push your brand to as many people as you can imagine without you having to break the bank. It offers you an unequal opportunity to build your much-needed traffic and brand awareness. In today's audio-visual society, it's really hard to deny the effectiveness of YouTube marketing. With YouTube marketing, your social reach will experience an unequal level of expansion, irrespective of your location in the world. YouTube takes your ad to the views of audiences overseas and increases your market reach. Do you doubt this? May I remind you that YouTube is the second largest search engine and the third-most visited website in the world. In fact, if you are not on the platform, you haven't reached the pinnacle of your digital marketing success. What's more, you have been missing the 1 billion people who have been coming online to watch hundreds of videos being uploaded every second.

ModCloth is one of the few online retailers who has harnessed the full power of the YouTube platform to increase their sales. This company was able to utilize this platform to run a successful media campaign, which increased their sales and awareness.

There's one more good thing about this platform; your content never dies. In fact, all you need to is re-purpose what you've already created without needing to spend much more time or investment on new equipment. With a good trick, you will get a great result in your YouTube marketing campaign.

## 1. Capture Attention

It's easy to get lost in the plethora of videos being uploaded on YouTube every minute. The competition is real. Do you have an idea of how many brands are in the world today, or how many new products are being created around the world every day? How about your locality, do you have an idea of the number of marketers and retailers who are also trying to push their brand on YouTube? Probably a hundred or a thousand. So, how can you stand out? Well, the answer lies in the creativity of your ads. Creativity is the secret. Do something that supersedes what your competitors are doing. Capture your audience. Think outside the box. The end justifies the means. It's of no use rushing to have an ad online when you can sacrifice more time to create something better. Do you remember the viral Volvo ad a few months ago? This video showed a popular actor and stunt guru, Jean-Claude Van Damme doing an epic split while balanced on two Volvo trucks moving in sync with each other. The ad did not only garner about 68 million views, but it also increased their sales by thirty-one percent. Creating a captivating video keeps your viewers glued to your Video content and you have just twenty seconds to do that. Furthermore, to create a captivating video, you need to carry out thorough research on the strategies adopted by your competitors; this will enable you to work from a fresh perception

This gives you an edge over them on the platform. Moreover, you can go in-depth on a subject matter, and you don't have to use a conventional approach. While creating your videos, ensure that you never compromise on the quality and creativity. Never forget!

## 2. Your Title and Description are Just as Important as Your Video

Do you know that the time spent by viewers watching a video is title, description, and tags and is as important as your video content? A misleading title or description is a turn-off and makes it highly unlikely that someone clicks on your video (as a result of your deception). Even if they do click on it, they won't stay to watch it for long. Why? It's not what they are searching for; it doesn't answer their basic need. A misleading title will make you lose the right (targeted) audience. It is worthless to spend much time developing a creative ad, only for your targeted customer not to see your ad when searching for specific keywords that define your content. The sad effect of misleading content is that it makes the YouTube algorithm to demote you. This is because the algorithm is designed to promote videos that viewers spend more time watching than those, they spend less time viewing. Although the standard limit for a title on YouTube is 100 words, it is advisable to keep your title as short as possible. The shorter the title, the higher the chances of visibility. However, your title must reflect the content of your video. A jazzy title might be fun, but it will hinder your videos from being seen when viewers search for keywords that relate to your content. The description for your video ad should be detailed and short. Remember people come online (on YouTube) to watch a video, and not to read. Your description should provide more information about your video. This makes it more searchable and also gives your audience a broader and deeper context for what they are viewing. You can also use the description space as an avenue to direct your viewers to your other social media accounts or website. This enables them to have a better view of your brand and also gain confidence through customer reviews of your product on your Facebook and other social media pages.

## 3. Make Your Video Ad Short

Have you ever heard of the golden rule? It's a basic principle that must be followed in order to ensure success. The rule very much applies to video marketing: under no condition should your video ad be more than three minutes. Never. Your video length has the power to determine the ability of your video to engage your targeted customer. In addition, it also determines the possibility of your targeted audience watching your video unto the end and understanding what you are trying to sell to them. To buttress this point, Wistia conducted research to determine the relationship between video length and average engagement. The results showed that average video views drop significantly after the first 2.5 minutes. You can choose to make a live video or an animation, the real deal is to make it short. A boring lengthy video on YouTube will get you nowhere, not even anywhere around the first YouTube pages. I would recommend you use an explainer video, as they have the potential to engage your customers more when compared to other types of video. It is well known to speed up conversion, hence increasing sales. This is because it increases user understanding of your product. Within three minutes, you can use the first few seconds to present the problem, after which you offer a solution to the problem, introduce your brand, and then try convincing your viewers why they should choose your product to solve their problems.

## 4. Be a Solution to Your Audience Problem

Your YouTube audience has needs, to which they desire satisfaction. They searched out your video content with basic keywords because the keyword holds the solution to their needs. They are interested in what you have to say to them. Most times they come online with a "blank" mind. No other alternatives. While some have, they just need a little conviction. You, as a YouTube marketer, need to be able to give them what they want, a solution to their innermost desire, while also been able to stay "true" to your own brand. No two audiences are alike. For instance, you specialize in beauty cream, a lady suffering from acne problems will search for "beauty cream" on YouTube; on the other hand, someone else searching for a brand that treats pimples will also enter the same keyword "beauty cream" or "beauty cream that treats pimples". This is two different audiences whose need varies, came for two different things, but whose answers lie within your brand; beauty products.

There is a need for you to find a healthy balance between what your audience needs and what your brand needs. This is key to how you market your brand to your audience. Also, remember,

YouTube is a global platform, not some local or regional platform; your content ad should have a global appeal. Someone in Africa should be able to watch your video ad and relate with the content.

## 5. Learn About Your Targeted Audience

Nothing beats the act of learning. How well you know about your audience determines how many followers you will grow over the years on YouTube. Poor knowledge of their basic information such as: watch time, demographics, age, and gender will definitely affect your expected result. As a YouTube marketer there are some questions you should get an answer to, to have a good brand marketing on YouTube. Ask yourself: What age is your audience? What age range watch your video most? 20? 30? 40? What's the gender of your regular viewers? Is it mostly male or female, or perhaps both fall into the same proportion? Where are your videos being viewed the most? Is it Europe, Asia, the

Middle East, or Africa? Strictly monitor the demographics and watch time using YouTube analytic tab. Most times, we might have an assumption of who your subscriber is and where they are viewing from, however affirming your assumption quantitatively will do you a lot of good. It makes it a win-win situation. If your assumption is right then you are on the right track and, if otherwise, you can easily adjust your content strategy to reach your target audience.

You can also use the comment section to get qualitative information about your viewers. The sections most times provide answers to the "whys" and "hows" that cross your mind on YouTube. In the comment section your audience relate their thoughts about your video content; sometimes it could be a destructive criticism – reading it is not always fun, however, the information you get in this section will be valuable for your marketing strategy in the future

## 6. You Have Just 10 Seconds to Hook Your Viewers

Yes. People do not come online to waste time to watch every video that comes their way. As short as 10 seconds might seem, it has enough power to determine the future of your commercials. So, begin your videos with an interesting hook. "Show the end result first". A striking result keeps your viewers glued, it strikes their emotion and makes people more interested to see how you achieved your results. Research has proven that about 20% of YouTubers drop off within the first 10 seconds. Within 10 seconds they can determine whether your video deserves a watch or click away. So, the first impression matters. This is why I will advise you to make the most of the most first 10 seconds. The best of your strength should lie there. Have you ever come across Cute Girls Hairstyles YouTube video (please take a look.) The first few seconds of their video shows off the result of the hairstyle they want to educate their viewers before an explanation?

Furthermore, to create an awesome first impression, never start your video with a bland and unimpressive introduction. It kills. The most climatic part of your video should be the first thing they see when they start watching. It's not a must you adopt "the end result first" thing. You can use stories to pique their interest. It works like magic, too. Believe me, people are naturally hardwired for stories. It could be a personal story or a well-carved fictional story; just ensure your opener stories relate to the subject matter. The secret is, if you start your video with a bang, viewers aren't going to want to leave your video. They will be glued to the video until the whole message you intend to pass across has been delivered to their subconscious mind.

## 7. Your Thumbnail is Your First Impression

Have you ever heard of the adage, "Never judge a book by its cover"? It really doesn't apply here.

Your 'cover' must be as good as your 'book', otherwise you are clicked away. On YouTube, first impression matters. It's like a beauty pageant. There are so many competitors who appear beautiful, but the most outstanding is selected. There are a thousand and one video ads that address the same needs you offer a solution to, so when your targeted audience enters a keyword, he doesn't just see your own video content in the search feed, he sees thousands. The difference between a visitor viewing your video and scrolling past it is your thumbnail. Your thumbnail won't increase your chances of being seen in search results and recommendations, but it makes visitors stop over and check your content. Customize your thumbnail. Make your thumbnail attractive. You can choose to use images pulled directly from your content, or perhaps use good photo editing tools to design unique thumbnails. Remember your thumbnail must be attractive. I mean more attractive than that of your competitors, and it should be indicative of what your video content is about. A misleading thumbnail is a huge turn-off.

## 8. Highly Watchable Content or Nothing

That's it. I know you feel this tip is obvious, it shouldn't be here; it is general knowledge. Yeah. So thought those who are in the lowest ranking of YouTube's algorithm. The pressure to increase the number of your subscribers and get more views can really be crazy when you are in the heat of it. Today, YouTube is full of clutters or permit me to say garbage; or video content people to click away after a 10 seconds view. It is really easy to feel as a YouTube marketer you can ride on your increasing popularity and post sub-par content on your channel. Trust me, you won't get away with it. You can't. The secret to standing out of the crowd of competitors is delivering quality always. Create the best of the best quantity and post on your channel. According to the words of Isaac Newton, *"If I have seen any further, it is because I have stood upon the shoulders of them that are before me."* Spend a good time watching the videos of your competitors, study them, do more research. I will advise you to also view videos of industries outside of yours. Note the intriguing part of their videos and think of how you can apply a similar concept to yours. I am not saying copying, I am saying applying creativity to do it better than them. For instance, if you are in the cookies business, I'd probably take a tip from my all-time favorite YouTube commercials and deliver something better than them. Remember, the higher the power of your commercials to elicit emotion from your audience, the higher the chance of converting them. Good things don't come easy. Drawing emotion from your viewers is not a walk in the park. You need to carefully plan out your script. Think, do a table read, think again, rewrite it, table read again, re-write it again until you are satisfied with what you have written. Mastering the art of scripting can catapult your videos to an entirely different level than you could ever have ever imagined.

## 9. Get Your YouTube Channel

Successful marketing on YouTube is dependent on the number of subscribers you have. A YouTube channel is the hub for all YouTube marketing. It gives video marketing a meaning. YouTube offers every user a channel; every upload you make public shows on your channel. Yes, your channel serves as your identity; your channel is you. So, the secret to gaining more subscribers is how much effort and love you put into your channel. Every video counts. Hosting all your video in one place enables you to develop a community around your public videos. People (viewers) keep coming back for updates. Remember your channel is your brand. Nothing turns off a regular viewer more than a digression from your niche. Think for a second how will you feel when you visit your favorite cooking YouTube channel for the latest update, only to see a video on car talk? Feel good? Definitely No. A digression is an abomination. It is in your best interest to stick to your niche. Every piece that makes up your content must fit well into the narrative of your channel. I will advise you to draw and compare your content plan with your channel narrative before putting the piece together. A group of high-quality videos on your channel will increase the number of views you have on your account, hence ranking you higher above others in your niche. This feat makes YouTube able to accurately target an audience that are or may be interested in viewing similar content. Remember, channel visibility is the key to successful marketing. Stay focused on building your channel and watch as your subscribers increase.

## 10. Personalize your YouTube channel

Yes, personalize your YouTube channel. Remember, your channel is you; your channel is your brand. Personalizing your YouTube channel is highly important. Choose a channel name that matches your brand; it doesn't necessarily have to be your brand name, it must really have to relate with your niche. This is because your channel name not only appears on your channel, it also appears under video titles when a search is initiated by a visitor. Viewers can see it under recommended videos. Your channel should have a sense of personality and be unique; be creative, however, you are not a Tv celebrity; Justin Bieber or Ellen DeGeneres. Putting your name in the channel title won't do much good. I will recommend you do a little Googling to be sure the name you adopt isn't already associated with a rival brand. However, there is a need for you to exercise caution in creativity, as the name you adopt really needs to be relevant. Apart from your channel name, your channel icon and banner also contribute to personalization of your brand. Your channel icon can be anything: your picture, a picture of nature, animal picture, or design. However, I will recommend you use a logo or well-made design. Using a logo or a design to represent your brand makes your branding recognizable. It distinguishes you from a thousand competitors who share the same niche as you.

## 11. Focus on Generating High Traffic Volume

What you offer and what your target audience is, they are likely using YouTube. The potential it offers you for exposure is extraordinary. With over a billion users, the potentials of generating high traffic are real. No thanks to the development of mobile technology, which has made mobile phones available at an affordable rate, virtually everyone has access to the channel. Unlike traditional cable network and television, they are not restricted by time or location to view your ad. I wouldn't be able to watch an ad campaign shown by a regular TV unless I'm at home or my office has a TV. But with mobile technology, I am good to go at any point in time; in the public transport, in the park, at the airport. My location doesn't make a difference. To reinforce my point, research conducted by Google in 2016 showed that six in every ten individuals say they prefer online videos to watching live TV. It means an ad on live TV will miss six out of every ten of its target audience. Start generating your traffic on YouTube now. A high traffic volume will lead to an increase in sales. Sixty-eight million views on the Volvo truck ad I wrote about in the previous point generated about a 31 percent increase in sales for Volvo trucks. It means an increase in traffic will definitely generate more. The higher the traffic, the better the expectation met, after all you didn't spend so much time doing a video. Adjust to garner traffic, you came to make money. Have you considered doing a video that showcases to your targeted audience how your brand addresses their needs? Imagine doing a video that shows how people living in a swampy area, especially Asia and Africa, can use your car brand without getting stuck in potholes or having the car engine damaged. Knowing fully well that people living in these areas are always conscious of the kind of vehicles they purchase. How about having a video that educates your targeted audience on a specific topic or themes they really want to be addressed about. I'm not saying just by topic, but a topic that is in line with your brand or niche. As a digital marketer of kitchen utensils, it is forbidden for me to do a webinar that addresses a car problem.

## 12. Make Your Video Highly Educational

As much as creating engaging video content is no walk in the park, sales content will bury your ad in the pool of competitors. You won't stand out. Your video needs to be educational i.e. help your targeted viewers solve their problems. Highly educational videos usually have the highest level of shares in social media. This is because educational videos (how to do) addresses their individual problems to which they want a solution for. It is best to craft a relevant educational video about the problem your business is solving rather than create a simple ad about your brand. This single action will not only make YouTube search algorithm ranks you higher than your competitors but will also make your target audience attracted to your proposal.

## 13. Viral Marketing Works Too

Your video has as many potentials to go viral as Jean Claude's Volvo truck ad. If you think sixty-eight million viewers is a negligible number, maybe you need to take a census on the number of people in your community. However, viral marketing is really about racking up millions of views; views are not tantamount to money. It is an approach you need to develop amongst how your targeted audience can spread information about your brand. Your content should so much strike the emotion of your audience such that they find themselves sharing the content via other social networks. There are so many ways you as a marketer can spark the shares that will increase the chances of being seen by millions of leads ready to close deals. For example, you can embed your video content within relevant blog posts. You can also share a link to your content video by a Facebook or LinkedIn group. Most times people who receive a YouTube video passed on from friends, colleagues, or relatives share the video with others (sometimes social platforms), hence creating a ripple effect. The key to virality is to deliver value to your targeted audience. According to Jonah Berger, in his book "Contagious: Why Things Catch On", he outlined six things that make a content (video ad) contagious: Social currency, Triggers, Emotion, public, practical value, and stories. Content that makes people feel like they are in the know will be shared widely. Achieving this is dependent on how many real emotions your video content injects into your targeted audience. However, considering the aforementioned, you must ensure your ad triggers your targeted audience to think of your brand; their thoughts must be in line with the context that aligns with the product you offer.

## 14. Boosting Your Search Engine Ranking Will Do You a Lot of Good

Apart from the fact that YouTube is the second largest search engine in the world, its videos are usually ranked high on Google search engines. Have you ever observed that when you search for some keywords on Google, you observe related videos on Google search pages? This proves that developing your video marketing strategy on the YouTube platform can generate your real SEO result. According to a study conducted by CISCO, by 2021 video will represent 80% of all internet traffic. This situation will encourage Google to rank sites that offer video content higher. Meaning for every keyword an individual presses into the Google search engine, there are more chances that video content will appear than text content. So, treat your YouTube video content the same way you treat your blog content, or you would have treated your blog content, if you had one, knowing fully well that the success of blog content is dependent on your level of consciousness to the use of SEO. Firstly, start by doing keyword research. This can be achieved by making a list of relevant topics based on what you know about your business. For instance, a business that deals with the sales of cars can include "certified cars", "pre-owned cars" or "secondhand cars" as a keyword. Good use of keywords pushes you to the top of the heap. Secondly, ensure you optimize your YouTube content by using selected keywords in the tag, description, and title of your videos. Also, remember that an optimized and super relevant video makes Google rank your video amongst its suggested video. Furthermore, including your YouTube content within your website or blog content can earn you quality backlinks which will also help to boost your ranking, raising you above your competitors.

## 15. Be Humble, Ask for Subscribers

The best way of measuring the success of your video content on YouTube is by looking at the number of subscribers you have. The more subscribers you have the more the possibility of having better sales on each video ad you upload on your channel. The best option for you is to grow the number of subscribers you have on your YouTube Channel. Have you considered asking people to subscribe to your content? Perhaps, maybe that's what you need for successful marketing. In the real world, many people will not just subscribe to your site because of the quality or value of your content. A flat out ask will not hurt you. Bury your pride. Ask your viewers to subscribe within your videos. You can bait them to do this by incentivizing subscription with a contest. This tactic works exceedingly well. It is in human nature to love free things. There are two basic ways you can employ to incentivize people to subscribe to your channel. Depending whichever you are more comfortable with. The first is to organize a contest on social media where you promote your business, set the guideline for winning a free branded shirt or a visit to your plant includes subscribing to your YouTube channel. Prominent YouTube creator, Disney Kitty, employed this strategy to grow her channel subscriber into five figures within the space of a year. You can draw viewers from Facebook and other social media channels by sharing subscribe links in your video's descriptions. This move will help you increase the number of your subscribers.

## 16. How About Developing Your Video as a Series

Do you have a set of YouTube content that goes around the same theme? I mean contents that go together. It could be a recurring weekly or bi-weekly educational content in a niche or a Webinar that revolves around the same theme? Whatever it is or whatever topic it may be, it would be cool if you grouped them into a YouTube playlist. Nothing increases the time viewers spend on your channel like binge watching. A series playlist keeps your viewers glued to your channel without having to manually search for your other content, all they need to do is to click into the next. I know what you are thinking; how will it increase my subscription growth as a marketer? Well, it makes people stay longer on your channel and gives them the intuition that you have a plethora of high quality. It will also keep your video content highly organized. Have you ever visited the BuzzFeed Tasty YouTube channel before? Please do. Take time to study their playlist page. You won't but notice how highly organized their contents are. Their content is grouped by categories: 'dinner', 'one-pot recipe', 'vegetarian', etc. It reeks of professionalism. Nothing turns off a viewer like a channel that looks unorganized. It's a big turn off

## 17. Set a Schedule and Post Consistently

In YouTube marketing, consistency is the key. To a new YouTube advertiser, it might seem difficult to keep up with a consistent content post, but the real deal is you won't get anywhere unless you are consistent with the rate at which you upload your post. A big time gap between each post is a NO. Even if your video has more quality than Oscar-nominated movies or the content is a million times better than that of your competitors, a month gap between each post will discourage your existing audience. It makes no sense if after putting in so much effort into designing your title, description, tags, and thumbnail to enable you to appear before your viewers, and at the end of the day you could retain them. What does it profit you? Subscribers are not going to stay if you don't update your channel or if there is an irregular pattern in the number of times you upload your content. For instance, you update your channel four times a week and then you take a month before you upload another.

To keep your existing viewers, it is best to set a schedule for all your posts. Choose whichever is convenient for you; it could be daily, weekly, bi-weekly or somewhere in between, as long as you can keep to it. I would suggest you communicate your upload schedule with your audience; this single act will keep them anticipated, they will have something to anticipate. Ask yourself, would you spend time watching your favorite TV show if you couldn't predict when the next episode would air? I wouldn't even waste a second of time. YouTube viewers have this same orientation.

They act the exact same way. If they don't know what's coming up, they won't tune in, they never will. Have a regular upload schedule and keep your viewers updated. Remember, how much audience you retain plays a significant role in increasing your future audience.

## 18. Engage Your Audience

The list of YouTube marketing tips is not complete without the option of user engagement. It is non-negotiable. Keep your viewers engaged. User engagement has the potential to convert your viewers into subscribers, from repeated views to subscribers. The comment section of your video offers you an opportunity to develop a personal connection with your viewers. The gap between viewers and subscribers lies in the level of personal connection you have with your viewers. In an engagement, you first of all need to encourage your viewers to comment in the comment section of your videos. This is one tip that contributed to the growth in the number of viewers Zoella has acquired on her YouTube channel. In her videos, she verbally asks viewers to respond to her questions in the comment section. You can adopt her style, or perhaps you can recommend it (comments) in your video description, "Please let's have your views". Furthermore, a like to comments in your comment section opens up the possibility of future interaction with viewers, especially those who want to have their comment featured. Viewer comments should not be neglected. Positive and negative remarks should be responded to professionally. YouTube's algorithm is designed to favor videos with more interactions. A longer comment section simply means more views; hence its algorithm pushes you up the rank. You can employ live streaming to increase your level of interaction with your viewers. Unlike regular videos, where you would have to wait for viewers to respond to the video you uploaded, through live streaming you can ask your viewers questions at the moment and receive instant feedback. Remember, cross-promotion between YouTube and social media platforms like Instagram and Facebook can actually boost your audience interaction. You can achieve this by posting links to your YouTube videos and posting to other social media with channel updates to keep your viewers updated in your latest uploads.

## 19. Collaboration Furthers Your Reach

Trust me, you won't regret this single act. Collaboration with other YouTubers in your niche gives you more reach than you can ever imagine. It causes a geometric increase in the number of audiences that meets your targeted audience profile. If you are into a confectionary brand, then search for top YouTube channels in the allied field. It could be with retail or a distribution firm with huge followers; contact them and see if you can feature them on your channel. Have you ever come across, Shawn Johnson East's YouTube video content before? Did you notice a large number of her YouTube following? It wasn't some form of magic or because her content is better than others within our niche who aren't doing so well. She collaborated with YouTubers that were in the gymnastic niche. This introduced other YouTube followers to her own channel, hence increasing her following. Collaboration works like symbiosis, both channels get an increase in views and follows. Shawn Johnson East's collaboration with Nile Wilson, a one-time British Olympic bronze medalist with over a million followers, increased her international reach. It also serves as an avenue to reach a new set of target audience. Collaborating with a YouTuber with a vast teen audience will get a large volume of YouTube follows

Collaboration sparks more interest and also increases loyalty. It makes prospect followers more interested in your niche or topic of discussion. It doesn't necessarily have to be a tutorial; you could make it an interview on topics that would be of interest to your targeted audience, perhaps an exciting contest or challenge.

## 20. Include Real People in Your Videos

Using real people for your video content rather than pictures or animation will do you some great good at increasing your number of followers. Don't get me wrong, pretty pictures are good, but it goes better with music than for a brand video content. Real people in video content makes the audience feel connected to the speaker in some way, Human craves human interaction; it feels more real. If you want your target audience to listen to what you have to say, get people in front of the camera. Someone who has the ability to smile naturally, act relaxed and looks good. Trust me, it works. It is known to cut through all the initial fluff potential consumers display. It doesn't necessarily have to be you doing the talk; you could get a friend, hire staff, or get a member of your team to do it. However, your choice depends on what you offer and your target audience. If you deal with a beauty product, get a beautiful person. A lady to sit in front of the camera. On the other hand, confectionaries will work better with teens and children. Whichever you choose, ensure they can act naturally and relaxed on camera. It has to look real. This single feat will make the message of your video seem more like a conversation than a marketing pitch

## 21. Your Audio Quality is as Important as Your Video

YouTube today is full of many crappy videos. Very unprofessional. Truth be told, the sound of your video is as important as your video itself, if not more than. Not so good picture quality can be overlooked, providing the content meets their needs, a poor video sound is an unforgivable sin. Imagine watching a video and you hear a lot of interference underground, or the sounds aren't coming out well, even though your video is on the largest volume. Youtubers are known to have poor tolerance for poor sound. They never come back. If you doubt this, visit YouTube and check the comment section of some videos. You will be surprised at the level of comments on the video sound. This is one thing many YouTube advertisers are missing; substandard recording equipment will result in bad video production. Shoot your video content in HD preferably and invest in a good microphone. Professionalism is needed here. Get standard equipment and a good location for recording. Remember, you aren't the only advertiser on the platform, it's a competitive ground, you aren't the only brand offering solutions to the problem of your target audience. Be wise. Be smart. Don't make your audience click you away.

## 22. Do YouTube Advertising

Apart from your YouTube channel, YouTube offers you an opportunity to get your content before your targeted audience through YouTube ads. This service comes at an affordable cost, compared to the value you stand to gain from this promotion. It's another great way of increasing the number of your subscribers. YouTube ads exist in various forms; sponsor cards, overlay ads, Display cards, Bumper ads, skippable video ads, and the non-skippable video ads. Each ad is a specific function, choosing which best soothes your content is the best way to go. For instance, to drive brand engagement, I would choose skippable video ads, not just because it reaches a wider audience but because I don't get to pay for the ads if the viewer watches for 10 seconds or more. It is a win-win situation. It offers you 5 seconds to captivate your target audience. Further, it fits well for product demos, how-to-do videos, and video testimonials. Overlay ads are a banner advertisement, they usually run along the bottom of a video, they are good for running reservation and sponsorship campaigns. Bumper ads give you the best result if your target audience come online through a mobile gadget. The maximum length it offers you for your content is six seconds; your concept needs to be carefully mapped.

However, the key to a successful YouTube

advertising is how relevant your product is. A content that is really engaging won't look like an intrusion; it makes viewers forget they are actually watching an advertisement. Remember it is an ad; every second counts, so keeps it short, hyper-targeted, and super entertaining.

## 23. Outbeat YouTube Algorithm with a Longer Video

Long gone are the days when YouTube pushes your video to all who subscribed to your channel. The search and recommendation engine has been basically switched to push newer channels to viewers. A big disadvantage to you as a marketer on the platform. It automatically reduces the chances of your subscriber or follower from seeing your posted content. But there is a trick to help trigger your YouTube SEO. Make longer videos. Extending the length of your video is another way to garner favor with YouTube's algorithm. According to Gwen Muller, vice president of content strategy at digital video network, content that lasts between ten to sixteen minutes are the sweet spot for YouTube. Amongst many things, the YouTube algorithm is designed to be watch-time-minded. The more time viewers spend watching your video content, the higher it ranks you up the algorithm. A 10-minute well-scripted video will push you up the YouTube SEO than a 4 minute or 2-minute video. Other Brands like Hyundai and Airbnb are beginning to pivot from shorter videos to a longer one. It's all about being smart, otherwise you won't get the results you seek. Famous lifestyle vlogger Remi Cruz, with over 2.4 million subscribers, had lengthened her videos from a few minute's content to about 20 minutes of video content. It's all about you demonstrating to the YouTube algorithm that your audience spend more time on the YouTube platform just because of your video. That's why they are online. Get it? This single feat retrains the YouTube algorithm to promote your video on its search engine and recommendation in order to generate more watch time

Moreover, a lengthened video offers you the opportunity to run multiple ads in the middle of one video. More money per view? Yeah, it increases your per video revenue. It raises the chances that someone will get your ad, hence you make more money for each video.

## 24. Live Streaming Videos

In the social sphere, engagement is the real deal and Live streaming does it better than prerecorded videos. YouTube's high-quality streaming makes it a better platform to engage with your audience live. A good way of impressing your target audience, hence making them stay longer on your video. It creates a high level of social interaction and garners a better connection with your audience. To ensure your viewers do not miss your live broadcast, you can advertise the event ahead of time, taking into consideration the demographics and occupation (likely) of your target audience. Doing a video when most of your target audience is likely to be asleep or at work with little to no time to watch is a big NO. It's a good idea to be conscious of their time zone before airing your broadcast; this allows you to have more viewers when your video is live, hence increasing your SEO rank on YouTube. Live interaction with your audience builds loyalty to your brand. You will have the opportunity to interact with them live, hence gathering valuable feedback on your regular videos

Furthermore, you can easily earn money on live stream by Enabling ads on your channel, however, it is not guaranteed all your viewers will see the ad.

# Chapter 4: Instagram Digital Marketing Tricks

Most times, digital marketers find themselves contemplating whether Instagram can serve their purpose of increasing sales, knowing fully well that it was originally created as a photo sharing platform for friends and family to socialize. Instagram is one of the most important social media channels around. Over the years it has proven to be the most powerful marketing tools for brands seeking to increase awareness about their product and expand their presence. The level of engagement Instagram offers, in terms of connection with your followers, is second to none. With over 72 percent of its users admitting to purchasing products whilst online, the results are hard to ignore. It is simple, visual and more attractive to the millennial-younger generation than any other social media platform today. If you have not joined the Instagram bandwagon yet, you do your brand great disfavor. With over 1 billion active users and about 500 million users coming online on a daily basis, rest assured that your ad will definitely get across to a great number of targeted audiences

The site goes beyond posting compelling photos of your products to the feed of your audience. You can create a profile that highlights your brand's vision and mission, show your products to your visitors, and capture leads and sales.

If you really want to get your business on the map, be known far and wide, you need to be on this platform. Instagram has become the hub where popular brands like Coca-Cola, Adidas, and innovative new brands, have been able to establish themselves in many households.

## 1. Be Strategic with Your Use of HASHTAGS

I know you have a good knowledge of how crucial and beneficial the use of a hashtag on your Instagram ad is. A recent study shows that including just one hashtag in a post can increase engagement by 12.6 percent. That's extremely high when considering the fact that it costs nothing to include a hashtag in a post. A hashtag is really useful for an ad. It allows people who are outside of your current followers but also fall into the line of your potential customers to discover your post, i.e. effectively expanding your brand visibility and awareness. Therefore, when users search for your niche, they will come across the relevant hashtags you are using, and this will lead them straight to your page. Hence, you gain more followers. In addition to this, you can encourage your followers to use your hashtag when they purchase your products or services. Creating your own hashtag also gives you dominance over your competitors in your niche. To boost the impact of your brand, you can pair your hashtags with a couple of promotional prizes. However, there is a need to apply caution when hashtagging. Most times, in a bid to keep up with our post we find ourselves hashtagging every seemingly relevant word we can think of even tacking, those that are not in any way beneficial to them for the particular ad in question. Remember, the key to letting the right people (your potential audience) see you is to use the right hashtag. To get the optimal results you can conduct brief hashtag research by typing in some words in the Instagram search bar. It shows you a comprehensive list of hashtags in use. Be sure not to select hashtags that seem to be "too" popular, or else you will get lost in the shuffle. Select the ones that are not too popular and are common among your competitors or partners. It's undeniable that hashtags come with myriads of opportunities such as increased brand awareness and sales conversion. However, using banned hashtags can eliminate any chance of you getting your post to your target audience. In fact, you might lose your long-term account. So, why risk such disappointment when you can easily prevent it. So, take the step to check any hashtag you want to include in your post.

## 2. Make Use of Instagram Stickers

In the last few years, Instagram Stories have

become the necessary ingredient to give your business a fighting chance. However, the sheer size of these stories can be quite daunting. So, how can your business stand out amidst the crowd? Well, the best way to give your business a fighting chance via Instagram Stories is to add stickers. Yes, it's quite amazing how you can create polls, add GIFs and emojis to give your stories a personal touch. So, why don't we explore the full potential of Instagram stickers and see the different ways you can spice up your Instagram Stories with stickers. There are basically ten essential types of the Instagram sticker. With each performing a specific function. They are Hashtag stickers, Mention stickers, location stickers, Question Stickers, poll stickers, Product stickers, music stickers, emoji stickers, GIF stickers, and date stickers. You can beautifully combine different stickers in the same story to double the benefits and maximize their impact. Creativity is needed in the application of these stickers to get your required result. Some of which are:

- *Drive sales to your latest products*

Think again if you are of the opinion that Instagram's new Product Stickers are just for raising awareness for your products. You should know that users can tap on them to learn more about the product, and also tap again to purchase the product on the product page. You can also add multiple products to give your audience a large variety to pick from

- *Ask for feedback and test ideas*

Emoji slide stickers, Poll stickers, and Question stickers are excellent tools for getting different types of feedback within 24 hours based on your preference. This helps you to relate to your audience, and it also helps to gauge their response to a new product or marketing idea. For instance, The Gap's Instagram Story uses an emoji poll to gauge their response while showcasing their products.

- *Kickstart an AMA to become closer with*

*your followers*

Facilitate Ask Me Anything (AMA) sessions with the Question sticker, and give your followers the opportunity to know you and your brand better. They will probably want to know about what your brand stands for and the new products you have in store for them. Let people know that you will only answer the best questions, and you will be amazed at the large response.

- *Distribute user-generated content and motivate others to create their own*

Never underestimate the power of user-generated content. By using mention stickers to tag the creator of the content, you can show your audience just how much you care about them. Better still, ask permission from your audience to directly share a post you are tagged in, and add a credit next to the mention sticker. This move encourages users to tag your brand in their story.

- *Add a soundtrack to create relatable content*

Music Stickers can help you set the right mood to effectively grab your user's attention. These stickers help you to get creative with your content - by playing a piece of your favorite holiday music or by lip-syncing along on video. What's more? Instagram lets you access different types of genres from popular artists on Spotify. Remember, showing you have similar taste in music with your audience will work wonders for your brand

- *Promote your branded hashtags*

Hashtags are a great way to get people talking about your product. More so, branded hashtags or event-specific hashtags can boost awareness for your events and encourage users to create content using the same hashtags. Integrating hashtag stickers in your Instagram story has a greater effect than using hashtags with Instagram posts. What's more? When your branded hashtag is filled with content from your fans, you can easily use the hashtag sticker to lead your audience to this gallery of content. Hence, your brand gains credibility

- *Tag locations of events you're attending*

Location tags are great for building networks with your followers and those in your respective niche. If you are attending a farmer's market, conference, or any other event, you can use the location tag to let your followers link up with you. You could also add specific instructions on where they can find you at the event.

- *Ask customers to choose between two products*

Want to learn more about your audience preferences while promoting your products? Then you need to incorporate the Poll sticker on your Instagram story. You can share the results when the voting is over, in order to encourage your users to purchase the product they voted for.

- *Make use of date stickers for a walk down memory lane or to hype up events*

Ever wondered why #TBT is a popular hashtag? Well, it's refreshing when you reminisce on past events and memories. You evoke a sense of camaraderie with your audience when you use date stickers to celebrate milestones and anniversaries. In addition to this, date stickers are great tools when you are counting down to a particular event. Attaching a date sticker to a behind-the-scenes video of a sneak peek photo lets them know much time they have left before the event.

- *Utilize the "Swipe Up" GIF sticker to garner more click-through from followers*

If you want to get your users to follow up and respond to your call of action, you need to use subtle methods to achieve your aim. Users, sometimes, need a bit of a push to take action, and the "Swipe Up" GIF is the perfect candidate for this job. GIFs such as "Swipe Up", "Follow Me", and "Check It Out", can call attention to the fact that your story contains a link.

- *Utilize the "Sound On" GIF to encourage users to activate the sound*

Videos play without sound by default on Instagram. Adding the "Sound On" sticker to make it clear that sound is included will spur the users to enable sound. In addition to this, it helps you captivate your audience's attention far longer than when you don't include the "Sound On" GIF

## 3. Show Your Ads When Your Targeted Audience is Likely to Be Active

Running your ad when your audience is likely to be online increases your chance of being seen. Ask yourself what times does your target audience likely come online. Every niche has its own targeted audience who also happen to have different active times. Post at the right time, having your targeted audience location in mind. For instance, if you are a clothing retailer, posting an ad in the early hour of the morning isn't a good idea. No one comes online to shop for clothes in the early hours of the morning, most especially Monday morning. Ask yourself, what is the likely hour of the day or day in the week will most of your target audience be on Instagram. That's the best time to post your ad. If you have a good idea about your audience, I mean in terms of demographics and other relevant attributes, it shouldn't be a hard thing for you to determine. If your audience is in China, Britain, and Nigeria, you need to post your ad based on their respective time zone. However, trial and error isn't a bad idea. Besides, you don't have to be online at the needed time, with lifetime budgeting, Instagram offers you an incredible opportunity to schedule when you want your ads to appear. This helps you to accurately target when your ad will appear in the feed of your targeted audience. If the lifetime budget doesn't seem a good option for you, you can make use of free ad scheduling tools to schedule your ads. Some of them are Hootsuite and Buffer. Remember, placing a good restriction on your posting frequency prevents your audience from been overwhelmed.

## 4. Study Your Competitors

Studying your competitors is a great way to stay inspired. The insight you are able to gather will help you to develop your marketing strategy and make you stand out to your target audience. Here you get to know what works well and what doesn't. Your Instagram post shouldn't be a carbon copy of that of your competitors but it's a cool way to draw plans and contents that beats theirs. look for the posts of those that have a great number of followers on Instagram and do a thorough research on what they are doing, what they are not doing, how they do their post, the time they post, and a mental picture of what their daily Instagram activity is like. Identify their core concept; their customer emotion driving force. It could be the kind of images they post, how they caption their images, their use of hashtags, their use of Instagram stickers, the way they market to their audience, the way their Instagram stories are structured, or perhaps the time they post their content. It could be anything. Sometimes it is little things that seem negligible. I will recommend this trick to you as a digital marketer on Instagram; if you observe there is a strategy you need to increase the awareness of your brand, but you seem to be struggling with, you can compare, note the differences between and learn what you can do better

For instance, as a fashion brand posting an image isn't a problem; the real problem lies in how the caption you use relates to your product or the quality of the picture uploaded on the platform. A product picture with the wrong caption will make your audience more confused. Take time to study them, pinpoint them, and improve on them. This step will give deep insight into your target audience's expectation. Remember, on Instagram, the basic difference between a successful brand and an unsuccessful one is the value of the content they post.

## 5. Run a Contest

The Instagram contest is the best to get more followers, develop an engaged audience, and grow your brand. People naturally love free things. Anything that carries the word free gets our attention in some way, even those things we really do not have need of. Running a contest is one of the best ways to encourage customer engagement. It draws viewers to engage with your brand. Someone has been scrolling away your post in the past will somehow click on it to know what you have to offer. Give away relevant gift, not prizes that have nothing do with your brand. Give out prizes that relate with your brand or niche. Examples of good options for prizes are gift cards to your store, free branded product, giving your followers an opportunity to try your products

If you are offering a week's supply of free branded towel or a bottle of wine, a follower will easily like and share your post as many times as needed to qualify. The process of joining your contest should be simple and straightforward. The contest itself shouldn't be so hard, otherwise it's a turn-off. It could be a quiz, puzzle, or a question that relates to your niche or brand. It shouldn't be too simple, rather it should be really engaging. The more they like and share your post, the more chances you have to be seen by a potential audience. Care needs to be exercised when running a contest; there is the risk of flopping and attracting the wrong type of people

However, if what you have is just a few followers, running an Instagram contest might be a loss to you. You need to consider the effort you put into running and organizing the contest in comparison with the returns you are likely to get. In a scenario such as this, you can partner with a business in the same niche that has a larger number of followers. This will expose you to a larger audience and gain you a good number of account followers and Instagram likes, shares, and ad engagement. For instance, as a marketer of a newly released soft drink, you can partner with a big restaurant with a huge following to organize a contest; qualification could be to tag or follow your drink. It's as simple as that. However, the level of engagement you get, do not let your contest run for too long. Most brand contests on Instagram run for a week. Followers are more likely to procrastinate, and perhaps forget to enter your contest while it is still on. The start and the end date need to be clearly stated

## 6. Have you considered Instagram stories?

What has Instagram stories got to do with your ad engagement on Instagram? Much in every way. It is the most amazing way to share your content on Instagram. It is the best way to generate leads. Studies have shown that stories help to increase brand engagement on the platform. It might not be directly connected to your ad, but it increases the level of your presence on the platform. Maybe you need to increase the number of stories you share on Instagram, at least one story a day, including your own story ad and see the level of engagement it will fetch you in comparison to engagement using other ad formats on the Instagram platform. Stories are the easiest way to get your followers engaged; this Is because they are usually located at the very top of your follower's feed. You use it to direct them to your newly published photos or videos. Occasionally you can create a giveaway for your Instagram story, post a story with promotional pricing on some of your products, make it a limited time offer, and then link the product page to your e-commerce website through your story.

The posting also offers your brand an opportunity to be featured on the Instagram Explore page. The explore page is the zone where Instagram users go to check new contents; you can imagine the level of exposure and engagement you will get on your post and others. It will be massive. So, start sharing engaging stories, I mean super-engaging stories. Remember the secret to your account being selected by Instagram to feature on the explore page is based on the number of accounts you follow and the number of posts you engage with.

## 7. Tracking Your Performance with Instagram Stickers

It's undeniable that Instagram stickers are a great way to get traffic, social proof, and engagements. In addition to this, you create more awareness for your brand with Instagram Stories. To get a better understanding of the effects of different stickers on your stories, it's important to monitor their performance over time.

And the best way to achieve this is to utilize Instagram's Insight to monitor your stories' performance. There's a section under the "Content" tab that's completely dedicated to stories on this platform. This allows you to gauge each story based on different metrics. However, ensure you use the right metrics. This is because you cannot optimize your performance on Instagram unless you have a good idea on how well your post and pages are performing. They really could be underperforming, in terms of the level of engagement and the number of customers converted through them. When you have an eye on the pattern of your follower's growth rate, you can gauge how the content you post is affecting things. Check out engagement rate, average engagement percentage of your total followers, and the engagement rate of each post. More so, you also need to track your URL click-through rate on Instagram (if you have one), measure how many people are clicking through to your URL.

## 8. Target Your Audience

With over three hundred million users who share over seventy million videos and pictures every day, rest assured that your targeted audience is here. Instagram, like Facebook, offer you an opportunity to be specific when targeting your audience for an ad campaign. You can determine the location, demographics, interest, age connections, age, behavior, lookalikes, and so on.

This ensures the right audience get your ad post. Most marketers on YouTube don't give the segmentation option a consideration, they just post their ad to a broad audience, hence resulting in poor engagement. However, there is a need to strike a good balance when targeting your audience. Inasmuch as it is good to be specific when targeting your audience, being too specific in your targeting options may end up resulting in a very few audiences seeing your ad. Our goal here is to ensure that the relevant people get to see your post. @mentions is another good way to directly target your prospect. Identify popular accounts, your targeted audience is following and @mention them in a relevant way, there are high chances that the mentioned account will report to their followers. I would also recommend you tag pictures taken at your business location; this single act strengthens the connection between the content and your brand especially when they get extra exposure among users that are browsing memories and events

Another way to get across to a potential audience is by generating leads from the comment section of your competitors. Find their unhappy and dissatisfied customers, pitch them, offer them your better solution to their problem. Unethical? Of course not. It is business. However, when reaching out to these people, do not be too pushy (being pushy is okay), but with an intention to really help them. Remember the words of Cary Vaynerchuk in regards to selling: "Selling is an act"

## 9. Share Your Customer Reviews and Testimonies

It is one thing to try convincing your followers that your product is awesome and it's the best buy they can ever get, it is a whole different thing when someone they really can relate to sings your product's praise. It's really an entirely different thing. Today, sales are no longer dependent on how good you are in advertising on social media; the vast number of marketers and the sale of substandard products has drawn skepticism from people to products sold online. In fact, today it is easier to get drowned in the noise of competition. Believe it or not, people trust each other more than they trust your brand, most especially when you are a new brand or trying to introduce a new product

I would say appropriate use of customer reviews will generate you more revenue. It's a sure way of assuring customers that your product is living up to the hype. Increasing the volume of reviews you publish on Instagram leads to a higher conversion rate. Collect testimonials and reviews from users who have used your product before and share the best of them on Instagram. The testimonials must be clear and written in a coherent fashion; it shouldn't appear as false or inauthentic otherwise you might end up making them confused. It will be most effective not just share them on your Instagram page but also display them on your business website or eCommerce store. This helps boost the pace of your audience conversion. However, never, never offer your customers any reward (including discounts) for testimonials about your product. It undermines the authenticity of your brand and largely erodes potential audience trust in your customer base

## 10. Join an Instagram Pod

Guess you are wondering what an "Instagram pod" means. An Instagram pod is a group of Instagrammers belonging to the same niche or similar, who share strategies and tips to help promote each other's ad content. Each member has some form of a useful tip, either by experience or by learning, which he shares with other members of the group. An Instagram pod is usually made up of between 10 – 15 Instagram users. They usually communicate via direct messages and most times when a member of the group publishes new content, they share them in order to increase the level of engagement of each post being published by members of their group. Joining a pod is strictly limited to an invitation. However, another way to locate and join them is usually through an Instagram themed group on Facebook. There are a lot of them on Facebook. Another way you can join a themed group is through networking.

## 11. Be More Focused on Engagements Based Content

Increasing your engagement and brand awareness level is not a factor of how many times you post promotional materials on Instagram. No, it doesn't work that way. It is dependent on how engaging your contents are. Most times we find ourselves constantly tempted to tell stories of how amazing and super your product is. It could sometimes piss a customer away. Rather than that you should incorporate your brand into your engagement content. Your branding could be anything; it could be your color, logo, font or anything that performs the function of brand awareness. It takes their mind off the fact that you are trying to push your brand across to them. A spot the difference post is a good example of engaging content; it keeps your audience focused on your brand without them being consciously aware of it. It doesn't look self-promotion but it actually is

## 12. Evaluate Your Field

Stand out of the picture and take a good look at your feed. Examine your Instagram stories, the video content you posted, the pictures and captions on your feed. Ask yourself, if you had been in your targeted audience's shoes, would you have been interested in the stories and posts? Would it have appealed to your emotion or per5haps move you to engage with the (your) brand? Instagram requires a lot of work, Creativity, strategy, and consistency. What you sow is what you reap. You can't put in little effort towards growing your brand awareness and expect the same result as someone who dedicated most of his time towards customer engagement. It doesn't work that way. Your major interest on the platform is to gain (or grow) followership who will be later converted into loyal customers; you need to invest much of your time publishing posts that will give your brand purchase credibility. It should be a mixture of stories, pictures, and videos in no definite pattern. Only ensure that it portrays the quality and reliability of your product. If it is to be a picture of a business or product, be sure the picture reeks quality. However, if it is a picture of nature or animal or what have you, ensure the caption reflects the function of the brand you are trying to introduce. Remember it's a competitive platform, and there are a thousand and one customers trying to get the same customer's attention. You really need to invest a good time curating your Instagram feed. The secret is to view your Instagram page as your business office and think like a potential customer. Would you have been interested in the page?

## 13. Give sponsored Ads a Trial

Compared to other social networks, Instagram has the most engagement. With over 500 million users on the platform, there are high chances that your target audience is on Instagram. Paid ads on

Instagram pays better than another social media platform. It is the best weapon of mass exposure. It brings your post to the feed of your target audience. With paid ads there are higher chances of being seen by your target prospect. The sweetest part about sponsored ads on Instagram is that you have absolute power to decide how much you will spend on them, you have the choice to decide whether you want to showcase a multiple ad or just one. You are no longer limited to individuals following your account. Your update is exposed to a whole lot of users at a fairly low cost (when compared to other social network platforms) provided they fit into your target audience. To get the best out of sponsored ads, use content that is really engaging, content your targeted audience cannot ignore. It is best to tailor it in such a way that it will be appealing to the demographics you are targeting. A sponsored ad targeted toward potential customers in China should be quite different from the ones targeted toward a southern American. A sponsored ad doesn't necessarily have to be new content; you can make use of the top post, most especially high performing ones. A sponsored ad doesn't necessarily have to be a photo, it could be a video, stories, stories canvas, carousel, etc.

## 14. Be Personal on Your Instagram Post

I know you opened a business account to increase your brand awareness and get more sales, but that doesn't mean all you should do online is promote and talk about your brand. Constantly feeding us with your company news, awards, office openings, and newly released products. Erase the mindset of using your Instagram account for solely business activities. Try creating a personal relationship with your viewers. A good combination of personal relationship and business relationship helps bring about complete loyalty of followers to your brand. Your brand really needs to exude humanity, establish an emotional connection with your audience. Direct your strength towards showcasing to your audience what your real passion is outside of work. It could be your own personal love of horses or racing, or perhaps the volunteer activity you do as a company. I might seem out of place, but deep down in the mind of your targeted audience, it shows them you care very much for a special cause or that you are doing your part in the community. If you work towards building a human and emotional connection with your Instagram audience, it will make you very much likable and at the same time develop a stronger brand loyalty.

## 15. Make Use of Free Instagram Tools

Like Facebook, Instagram offers you an amazing opportunity to view statistics on how your followers are engaging with your data, an accurate breakdown of the demographics of your Instagram followers, their gender, age, and most active hours. It gives you a specific and detailed insight on the number of impressions you earned by virtue of your post and what your top post was. The insight you gain through the use of these tools helps you to re-strategize and re-plan.

Contents that do not drive a good level of interaction from your viewers can be discarded, allowing you to focus on developing contents that drive engagement. You need to ask yourself why those contents are not driving the engagement you require; could be your targeted audience do not get emotionally connected to your post? Does it confuse them? Are they on another time zone and they don't get to see it? You really need to find an answer to this question and what you need to do to improve on it. Engagement is our core goal here. A category of post that never ceases to grab the attention of an audience is the product teasers. Maybe you should give it a trial for a week and use the Instagram tool to gain insight into how well your audience reacted to it.

## 16. Don't Be Pushy

Being pushy or aggressive on social media turns followers off more than it converts them. Have you heard this before? No, I guess. If you are too pushy with your ads, trust me, followers will drop away like flies. In fact, it is the surest way to turn them off. If all they see on their news feed is your brand, you will be surprised at the steady decrease in the number of your followers. If you play your cards well, you can advertise effectively without annoying or scaring Instagram users off. Take a cue from Gilt Man's Instagram page; you will observe that most of his posts don't really appear as if he is trying to sell a product but trust me it's bait. Imagine being offered a free app where followers can shop all of its brand inventory. What does that look like to you at first glance? An advert? Of course not. Sometimes the brand offers the viewers about 70% off discount for some selected products while also displaying other items that are available for purchase. This kind of ad works well because then they aren't pushy (they don't appear to be pushy), they appear laid back. Tease your followers with brand images in order to download your app and shop around. Additionally, you can also offer them a discount to entice them into purchasing your product. Starbucks uses this trick to gain more customers. Most times they announce seasonal drinks using sharp imagery; these efforts tease the customer into buying your product and they will be more likely to pull the trigger and buy something. At worst they will likely engage with your post by sharing, liking, or commenting on it.

## 17. Make Use of User-Submitted Photo

Here is another great way to increase your follower's engagement. Followers tend to flow better with user-generated content than one created by the business; they feel represented, as it speaks to their emotions. The fact that it is unpredictable and authentic gives it a more reliable means to engage your followers. It's a win-win situation for both you and your followers. It reduces the stress of generating new content while, on the other hand, it serves as an avenue to increase their own following. To get a better idea on how to leverage user-generated photos, check out cosmetics brand Mac's user-generated post. They make use of tons of user-generated content to show off their products on Instagram; observe how they tack the hashtag and tag the user in the selected image. You can make it look competitive by attaching incentive as a reward to whichever user-generated content is selected. Trust me, you will be surprised at the level of participation you will get from your followers. GoPro is well known for this act; the brand features a photographer every week. However, you need to exercise wisdom when choosing pictures you want to post. You should be able to find answers to whether the picture fits well with your brand image or does it contradict it in a way. Is the picture appropriate for your target audience or followers? You really need to be sure that everything you are posting is in tune with your brand message. It has to be of high quality, intriguing, and unique.

## 18. Branded Hashtag is a Good Option.

A branded hashtag is a great way of increasing instant engagement. They are a great way to build interest about your product. More so, branded hashtags or event-specific hashtags can boost awareness for your events and encourage users to create content using the same hashtags. It is highly interactive. It offers users an opportunity to easily access all posts relating to your brand on Instagram. Check out Red bull branded hashtag #itgivesyouwings; the tag carries over 299,612 posts. A click on their hashtag will expose me to all the posts with the hashtag. Making use of a hashtag that your company and other users can easily search for is basically free advertising, at no cost. To make it more interesting, you can make use of a slogan or phrase that associates with your brand or that you are well known for as your branded hashtag. For instance, Coke makes use of #ShareACoke as its branded hashtag on Instagram; a click on the tag will expose you to all their previous posts with the same hashtag. Imagine the level of exposure you will have if someone who has huge following posts a picture using your branded hashtag. Massive. Moreover, you can always select pictures you may want to consider for reporting on your own business page. In addition, integrating hashtag stickers in your

Instagram story has a greater effect than using hashtags with Instagram posts. What's more? when your branded hashtag is filled with content from your fans, you can easily use the hashtag sticker to lead your audience to this gallery of content. Hence, your brand gains credibility

## 19. Engage Online

If your brand is new, you can leverage engagement as a means to grow your followers. For instance, an hour engagement per day with popular handles within your niche is also a good way to get noticed. Comment on their post, like and share them. This way you find yourself steadily gathering followers. You can also reach out to influencers who have a large number of followers that fall into the category of your targeted audience. Get them to interact with you about your brand. It could be an organized lunch meetup, where you share that you are having lunch with a said person, get them to do likewise. It's all about meeting the right person, getting the right exposure. It's a who you know thing and how many followers they have. It also involves how well you interact with brands that are very similar to your target audience.

## 20. Run an Instagram Ad to a Landing Page

One of the most reliable tricks to drive sales for your brand through Instagram is by designing an ad for your brand that links directly to your website or eCommerce store. All it takes is a click, and they are right on your website viewing all your amazing offers. Instagram allows you to add a CTA and click-through link to your ads on its platform, a unique feature it denies for other kinds of post. Post a couple of high-quality pictures of products you want to sell to your target audience with an appealing description or call to action. Your description must sound professional and convincing enough to make your audience interested in seeing what you have to offer. Urge them to buy your product. Remember, we are not been pushy, we are urging them, so they click through to your website, and then get them converted. The best way to get more click-through to your landing page and maximize sales is a limited time offer; make it time bound. You will be surprised to find them making orders before the stipulated closing date. You can also discount your ads for some of your products. You see, people love to be cajoled, to be persuaded; give them a reason why they should buy or act now rather than take action later. It's all about being smart. On the other hand, if you are a service provider, you can also create an attractive offer, that you can give out in exchange for potential lead information. You could offer them a free consultation or professional assessment. However, you must note that the secret of the success of your ad is dependent on the page you send your potential customer to; a crappy landing page is an unpardonable sin. If your landing page is not optimized (taking into consideration mobile users) for conversion, trust me, you will see little to no return on the money you invest in advertising.

## 21. Be Coupon-wise

Truth be told, Instagram is a passive platform. People come online without specific intent. They just scroll through their feeds without having any basic purpose in mind. Most times they idly do it to pass away time or to keep up on the latest update. Mastering the skill of moving your Instagram viewer's emotion from a passive to an active state will help boost your sales performance over the weeks. It's simple but requires a good strategy. All you need to have in mind before posting content on Instagram is, your content has the power to bring them out of their passive mind and make them active viewers. How do you do that? Promotions. Nothing moves Instagram users like promotion. It's like a bulb in their darkness. Post a product photo and highlight on the photo or preferably beneath a coupon code. To get the best of this you can target occasions like Black Friday or perhaps the Superbowl service. During these periods, more people are likely going to want to take the offer while also purchasing your product. However, caution needs to be exercised when offering coupons. If you're constantly offering out coupons, it makes it appear like you are cheapening your product in your customer's eyes and this tends to affect their demand for your product

## 22. Offer at Point-of-Sales for Following

Having a great list of followers means you have more viewers to show your brand product to. This increases the number of your sales. For instance, a brand that has a million followers to show its product to will have more sales than a brand that has just a few hundred. Apart from partnering with influencers or other YouTube creators within your niche, you can also make your target followers follow you by offering a certain offer to them at your point of sales, only if they can prove to you that they are following you on Instagram. You can get signage in front of your store, saying, "Special offer for followers on

Instagram". It could be a 10% discount or lottery. You can imagine how many people will follow your Instagram account, before stepping into your store. This trick works well for retail customers. With them, it's quite an easy thing to set up; just have them show evidence that they are your followers and then you reward them with an offer. Satisfaction will make them tell someone else, who will also tell someone else, and also pass the information to someone else, and then your accounts keep growing geometrically.

## 23. Show Your Audience Your Product in Action

Pictures of your products are a great way of Advertising on Instagram. According to Antonie de Saint – Exupery, 'If you want to build a ship, don't just ask people to gather wood and do not assign them responsibilities and work, teach them to long for the endless immensity of the sea"

Customers easily relate better with pictures of the product in action than if it were just a post. However, pictures of your product in action will get you a better rate of conversion. Consumers relate better with pictures showing someone using your products, most especially if the person in the said picture is a celeb or someone of importance within the circle of your target audience. For instance, if your product is a race canvas or a race kit, imagine what result you will get if you post a picture on Instagram of Usain bolt or a well-known athlete within your community racing with it. It will be explosive. It puts your target audience in the mindset of 'I could be this person'. However, if you are a new brand, you don't have to break the bank to achieve this feat; you can also make use of anyone provided they fit well into your plan. You wouldn't want to post a picture of an obese person racing with your kit. No, that's dead on arrival. Moreover, in a way, it enlightens your audience on the various situations in which your product can be used or ways in which it has an edge over that of your competitors.

## 24. Reach Out to Local Accounts on Instagram

There are a thousand and one local accounts on Instagram that focus on a specific city, town, or state. Most times they publish photos of popular local spots, businesses, tourist sites, and experiences in a geographical area. People in their targeted community have them as a source of an update. You can make use of them to reach out your target audience. Identify the accounts that have a large following and reach out to them to visit your business and post a review about it. It works well if your business is service-oriented, like a spa or restaurant. You can reach out to them to pay you a visit and let them have a first-hand experience of your service or product. A good review of your brand on their Instagram page will drive local dwellers to patronize your brand. Most times these accounts usually have online publications and newsletter they send to their subscribers. Featuring you on their newspaper or on their local blog post and newsletter will increase your business awareness in your targeted location. When local Instagram account people have come to trust over the years, it tells good things about you, it makes your brand seem reliable and approachable, deep within your targeted audience, it becomes humanized as a valuable contribution to the community.

Reposting contents of the local Instagram account in your targeted geographical area is also a good way to get noticed. They may mention your "shout out" on their page, and this will enable you to reach their followers and your targeted audience in the local community. With time your firm becomes humanized to them. They will see you more as a friendly neighbor rather than as a business after sales

## 25. Make Your feed Shoppable

You know that most people don't come online to shop or look for a product, they come online to keep themselves busy. It takes really great work to catch their attention, and a good strategy to convert them. Linking your Instagram to your website page is a good feat since the potential audience can easily have access to shop for your other products and get more accustomed to your brand. However, only a little percentage of people will make it to your bio to click and visit your website. That's how passive it could be sometimes. Besides, you cannot link to more than a page at the same time; this leaves you with the choice of making your link the same at all time or you change it every time you publish new content, both of which are not really an ideal situation. It is a good idea is to make their shopping experience begin from your Instagram feed. Hav2Have and Curalate's Like2Buy offers you an opportunity to achieve this. They are well-designed monetization tools you can use to give your target audience the best experience whilst on your feed. How does it work? They help create a page that perfectly replicates your Instagram feed. This allows your audience to get needed information of the products featured in the image by simply clicking on photos that strike their interest. It makes it easier for you to display multiple products without worrying about creating links for each product; a link is enough to link to your bio, which serves as a hub for all your products.

## 26. Include a CTA to Your Bio

The Instagram bio is the most underappreciated part of Instagram. It is usually regarded as an afterthought -a line about the company that you hurriedly fill out when you first opened your business Instagram account, forgetting that your bio is as important as your post, if not more important the later. Your Bio is a digital real estate that welcomes curious viewers to your profile, conveys important information about you and your business. Your Instagram bio is where visitors become customers. It has to be attention-grabbing. Imagine what effect adding a CTA on your bio will have to the level of conversion you will get. Massive traffic and conversion. Your bio is the most perfect place to have a CTA. The CTA serves as a complimenting factor to a well-constructed, emotional driving Bio. There will be an increase in the amount of traffic you will drive from your Instagram account to your website or eCommerce store. Use active language to move customers to action: Add "Click this link to shop with us", "Subscribe now", "Register now", "Shop with us" to your bio. A good CTA is one with the power to persuade your audience to do as you wished. If your firm is a service provider, you can display your email address to move people to get in touch with you for a discussion. You can give a quick check at Hello Fresh Instagram's bio, observe their skillful use of a convincing CTA to offer a discounted trial to new customers. One or two CTAs are okay.

## 27. Encourage Your Followers to Turn on Post Notification

Over the years, Instagram has made a lot of changes in the way it orders its users feed. The post notification feature can serve as an important tool for businesses to increase engagement with their followers on Instagram. Most times it could be really hard work, getting your target audience to see your content, especially followers who do not really interact with your post on a regular basis. The best way to ensure your followers get to see all your published content is to encourage them to make use of Instagram post notification features. They will receive an update every time you post new content. This tool will definitely help your brand increase its level of engagement with followers on Instagram. Once a new post goes live, the notification feature sends a push notification to all your followers. Hence, increasing the chances they will likely see it and interact with your brand (as expected) rather than just scroll past it in their feed like they normally would. The post notification feature is the easiest way to boost your organic reach. It works just like an email newsletter. To encourage your followers to put on their post notification feature, you can promote it across other social media platforms, where your brand has a presence. You can also use the contest as a way of enticing people to subscribe to post notification. How? Announce your organized contest in advance; people will be highly interested in when you will post so they can increase their chances of winning the contest. Make it a top 5, or top 10 things; "top ten to comment", "top five to like", "top eight to share", or" top five will get a 50% discount". It will be beneficial if you make it an offer or discount that expires.

# Conclusion

Social media is your best bet to boosting your visibility, increasing your brand awareness and converting a good number of leads hence making more sales. This accounts for why over 97% of marketers are making use of social media. However, doing it right is what gives you an edge and make you stay above the game, remember you are one out of over a million businesses making use of social media platform as a means of reaching out to targeted customer. Your key to excellence is the digital marketing tricks you use for your ad, utilizing the latest trend gives you faster organic growth and enables you to reach out to your targeted audience more effectively. So, take the step to achieve financial freedom through these tips and strategies.

www.ingramcontent.com/pod-product-compliance
Lightning Source LLC
Chambersburg PA
CBHW030514210326
41597CB00013B/900